THE ADVENTURES
OF MR THAKE

The
ADVENTURES
of
MR THAKE

J. B. Morton
(aka Beachcomber)

Published 2008 by Old Street Publishing Ltd
28-32 Bowling Green Lane, London EC1R 0BJ
www.oldstreetpublishing.co.uk

ISBN 978 1 905847 17 4

10 9 8 7 6 5 4 3 2 1

A CIP catalogue record for this title is available from the British Library.

Printed in Great Britain by Clays Ltd, St Ives plc

Contents

Introduction

THERE are men who bear upon them so unmistakably the stamp of their own country, and do so unwittingly reproduce in their actions and in their conversation, in their dress, their habits and their general bearing, the most widely known characteristics of their kind, that they move through our lives to an accompaniment of tolerant laughter. Their most pronounced follies endear them to us. They are, of their own nature, a caricature of a nation. No hatred can attach to them, even for their most ponderous imbecilities, since the clue to their characters is a simplicity that disarms all argument, and a primal innocence that is very dear to God.

Of these is Mr Thake, whose acquaintance I made some three or four years ago, and whose letters to me are here collected between covers for the first time. I have not presumed to edit even such of these letters as were obviously written under mental stress; and I have refrained from trying to explain his actions. Comments I have restricted to the minimum, since it is my belief that you will find the whole man in his letters.

I owe a double debt of thanks to the Editor of the *Daily Express*; first, for his courtesy in extending to my friend the hospitality of his columns; secondly, for permitting this reprinting of the letters.

I desire also to refrain from thanking Prodnose for his fatuous suggestions and irrelevant criticisms. It is in spite of his perpetual hindrance that the work has been brought to an end.

BEACHCOMBER

❖ I ❖

THE RIVIERA
AND AFTERWARDS

MY DEAR BEACHCOMBER,

The weather is very fine here. Yesterday I saw Tom Robinson, who, curiously enough, was lunching near me. I last saw him at Richmond – or was it Kew? – one day, two, or it may be three, years ago. We did not speak, as he did not recognise me. So perhaps it was not Tom after all. Who knows? Most people go to the Casino here when they are not doing anything else. When they are, there are less of them there than at other times, as you may well imagine. I have run out of cigarettes, but hope to be able to buy some here later at a tobacconist's shop – or whatever they call it here.

There is a lady in my hotel with a dog, who is rather like Mrs Phipps – the lady, I mean, of course – except that she is older, and is, they say, dumb, which of course, Mrs Phipps is not. If you see Barlow tell him he can use my clubs whenever he wants. I enclose some French stamps of twenty centimes for his boy. They are not very rare, I fear, but may please him. I can see the Casino from my room when the blinds are up, but the bathing is very crowded. They say there are crowds of English here, and I can well believe it, for I have seen them.

I am going for a drive now to some place I was told about – I forget its name, but it's supposed to be very pretty.

Yours ever,
O. THAKE

P.S. Tell Saunders to send out my flask.

As you will see from the above address, I have come on here from Monte Carlo. The train journey was not as tiresome as I expected, but I was glad when it was over. I have a pleasant room here, and I learn from the register that I have just missed the Walkers – I think you know their mother – her husband, their father, of course, was a colonel in some regiment during the war – the Staffords, I think. Well, anyhow, they left here yesterday, so I shall not see them here, unless they come back. I think there is polo here, or at any rate golf. But either here or at Nice I think there is polo. Now I come to think of it, I saw a number of ponies being exercised as I came from the station – but they may have been ordinary ponies. I heard from George yesterday. Curiously enough, he is at Horsham.

I was able to buy an English novel at the station. I forget who it is by. You may have read it. It has a shortish title and was about a seaside place somewhere. Not very good, but, at any rate, written in a language one can follow. I have been told I ought to go to Nice for the Festival, or whatever it is called. I must get out my maps, since I have become a veritable globe-trotter!

Yours ever,
O . THAKE

P.S. Tell Saunders to send out my panama.

4

I have finished the novel I was reading, and Mrs Warren has very kindly sent me out one or two old copies of magazines. These I exchanged for the "Lancet" with a doctor who is here – called Walters – quite a nice fellow, but Welsh. I'd no idea there were so many people abroad. One sees them wherever one goes. By the way, I see that a man called Graham has been appointed to a curacy at Northampton. I wonder if it is young George Graham, whose sister married Ted. He had thoughts of going into the ministry, but I fancy he entered the Stock Exchange instead, in which case this must be some other Graham.

I shall not stay here long, as I want to see the Festival at Nice. They say it is a typically Continental affair, with flowers and things.

There is quite an important politician here – I forget his name – he was on some kind of Commission of Inquiry during the Boer war. The ladies make a great fuss of him, and I think he supplies the hotel with more news than all the newspapers. Tell Hammond that he was wrong about the word of eight letters. A ventriloquist who is here gave me the right word, which I am sending in today. Poor old Charlie! I suppose you have seen the sudden drop in Enamels. He had quite a bit invested, I'm afraid.

Yours ever,
O. THAKE

P.S. Tell Saunders to send out my sponge-bag.

5

Here I am at last, after the journey. I find myself in the midst of the carnival spirit. Pleasing young women bubble over with high spirits. I bought a flower from one this morning, since everybody does this. It is hail-fellow-well-met here. The Penders are stopping at my hotel. It's four years since I have seen the boy. He has grown. My flask has arrived, also the tablets you were good enough to send me. I am sleeping better, but the dancing continues until very late. I have run out of stamps, but it is no good sending to England for those, is it? Anyhow, they tell me the concierge has some. And if he hasn't, I expect his wife has. These people always have. That is one thing I have learned by coming abroad. I find I am able to make myself understood in the shops by talking English. Some people talk French, but I think that is a pose.

The Carnival! You will want to know about it. Really it is very difficult to describe. There are vast crowds, all throwing flowers. One does not quite know what it is all about, but if you laugh and throw them back, you are all right. Of course, there is no horse-play. It is all just fun. A duchess was pointed out to me in the thick of it, but there are many of them here, and one takes no notice. I am told that they practically live here, on and off. I brought my new skis here, and wandered about looking for the places where they do this, but couldn't find them. Apparently there are no winter sports here – at least, not in that way.

Yours ever,
O. THAKE

P.S. Tell Saunders to send out my patent button-hole fastener.

This is very different from Nice. For one thing, it is much colder. I looked forward to some sport, but I very stupidly left my right-foot ski in the train, and so am left with one only. I have written to the authorities to recover it, and meanwhile a man here has offered to lend me a pair of skates till the other ski arrives. I have bought a small book on tobogganing, but it is written in German, so I can only understand the pictures. I was introduced to an actor here last night in the smoking-room. We talked for a while about "Hamlet". He seemed very silent for an actor, but some friend of his told me later that he is busy studying his part in a new revue. So he may have been preoccupied.

I have been on the rink, but I have come back, as it was very crowded with people taking photographs of each other. My actor-friend had no camera, but very patiently allowed them all to "snap" him. I am told that many of these photographs will appear in the newspapers in England, if they are good, and if the people here don't object. I happened to be standing near Lord Hulber's goddaughter, and a man came up and said to his companion, "With friend – add that, Joe." It was probably some game. She looked most annoyed, so I suppose they had won. Then a film-photographer asked some working people to make a big mound of snow outside the village. He kept telling them to hide while they worked as it was meant to be an avalanche. This must have been to amuse some children. He was very angry because a spade came into the picture.

Yours ever,
O. THAKE

P.S. Tell Saunders to send out my deck-chair.

Tell Saunders he has sent out the wrong hat. The Fentons are here, and have persuaded me to send to the nearest town for a horse. I suspect them of pulling my leg, as usual, as I have not noticed anybody riding here. Indeed, I do not know whether one could ride with any degree of comfort, since there is a good deal of snow. However, I have sent for the horse, and if the worst comes, as it well may, I can send it back to where it came from, without exposing myself to the ridicule of having made use of it in public. I have no time for more, as I am to be one of a tobogganing party on the mountain side.

Yours ever,
O. THAKE

P.S. Tell Saunders to send out my riding-switch, in case.

A Mrs Wrapper, an actuary's wife whom I met in Monte Carlo, told me I ought to see the Pyrenees. So I determined to go off into the wilds. Three young Oxford men very kindly told me where to go, and gave me many tips for the journey. When I learned that Biarritz was a lonely place, high up among the snow peaks, I smelt adventure. Also they told me that the inhabitants are very primitive. So I procured a revolver, secondhand, from a poulterer, donned my oldest clothes, stitched some money into my coat lining, and set out. At first it seemed pretty plain sailing –

an ordinary train journey. But I dismounted some miles from Biarritz, deeming it wiser to approach it under cover of night. As I drew near what looked like a street, I heard singing and music, and guessed that I had stumbled on some old native music.

Imagine my surprise when I found myself in a big, fairly civilised-looking town. The sounds I had heard came partly from a "pension," where a gentleman was singing "The Minstrel Boy," and partly from what I take to have been a cabaret, where – of all tunes – "Bye-bye Blackbird" was being played. And in place of natives whom should I see but the Scruttons, the Blands, the Holloways, and a number of other friends. Also a sprinkling of well-known society folk. I felt rather a fool in my old rags, with the revolver grasped firmly in my hand. How they laughed at me, thinking it was a practical joke – especially when I asked where the Pyrenees were.

Yours ever,
O . THAKE

P.S. Tell Saunders to send out my tie-press.

Hotel Gaga
Paris

I went last night, in company with Mr Thomson, old George Thomson's son, to a kind of revue at a place of entertainment in the Place Pigalle. We had dinner first in a smaller restaurant in the vicinity, and Thomson told me about his new plan for sending braces to the native tribes somewhere in the wilds – I forget the name of the place. We then repaired to the revue, which was of a somewhat startling nature.

The young women of the chorus, attired in a minimum of clothing sang at a great pace, and danced. There were a number

9

of women in the audience – a fact that made me blush. I could not follow the plot, nor much of the dialogue. Thomson laughed a good deal, but would not explain the jokes to me. He must be quite a tolerable French scholar, as I noticed that all the natives laughed when he laughed. One young woman handed me a bell attached to a coloured ribbon. Apparently I was intended to keep it. At all events, I have done so, not without misgivings. One gets into this kind of irresponsible mood in Paris. When the show was over we went to a café near by, and I had a glass of grenadine, which, I am told, is almost the national drink. The actress who had given me the bell was there, but I did not like to offer to return it, for fear of offending her.

I enclose my photograph.

Yours ever,
O. THAKE

P.S. Tell Saunders to send out my address book.

❖ II ❖

ON BOARD THE
S.S. LUTETIA

My Dear Beachcomber,

No wonder this vessel is called the Lutetia, for, indeed, it is like a floating palace. I can hardly believe I am at sea, except when I climb on deck and note that neither behind nor in front nor at the sides is any land visible – an impossible situation anywhere but in mid-ocean. Downstairs there are golf courses, dance-rooms, casinos, and tennis courts. It is rather a difficult matter to keep fit on board, but a Mrs Redpath, who is travelling for her health, recommends a cold plunge every morning, and a brisk walk on the deck. I notice in the list of passengers the name Scamble. It may be Dick Scamble, although I fancy he spelt his name Scambell.

The sailors are very jolly. I asked a group of them to sing a shanty the other day, but they only laughed. I think they were shy. I sat next to a man in an old Brambsleighian tie at lunch yesterday. I told him I had friends at the old school, but it turned out that he was an American whose wife had bought the tie because she liked the colours. He said he was at school at Omaha, and we discussed "O. Henry!" a book which I have never read. I must keep fit, and the cold baths are so crowded.

Yours ever,
O. Thake

p.s. Tell Saunders to send out my dumb-bells.

p.s.s. It doesn't matter. They wouldn't, of course, reach me before disembarkation.

We have had a very jolly ship's concert. I was very much flattered at being asked to take the chair. There was a good deal of pleasant singing, including a song that I have not heard before, called "Until". It was encored many times. I also enjoyed a recitation by a Mr Purbright, a young banker, entitled, if my programme reads aright, "Bloody Joe of Frozen Gulch". In announcing this I lowered my voice, as there were ladies present. But cries of "Speak up!" considerably embarrassed me. So I spoke louder, but omitted the adjective. We all joined in the choruses, particularly that of a fine hunting song, sung by a Mr Wisp, who, by the way, knows Scarborough well, and has actually called on the Grahams there. Isn't the world a small place?

I passed a vote of thanks, and they demanded a song. I saw that I ought to pay a compliment to America, but I really could not think of their National Anthem, so I gave them a song that I gather has been pretty popular there for some years –"No, We Have No Bananas". In this song I was accompanied upon the piano. It roused much laughter. So persistent were they in their demands for an encore, that I gave them my imitation of a cat lapping up milk. You will remember how it used to amuse the Lomax children – especially Winnie.

Yours ever,
O. THAKE

P.S. Tell Saunders to send out by express messenger the score of "The Belle of New York", which I have promised to an American on board.

A most extraordinary adventure has befallen me. Last night, as
you know, there was a full moon. Well, after dinner I was
strolling on the deck, when I came upon a young woman leaning
over the railings at the side of the ship. I was about to pass on,
not, as far as I could recollect, having been introduced to her,
when she turned and exclaimed on the beauty of the night –
afterwards begging my pardon for having taken me for someone
else. I raised my hat and paused. And then, somehow, we got
into conversation. When I told her I was travelling for pleasure
she sighed, and said how nice it must be to be as rich as that. She
then asked me to decide a dispute as to the colour of her eyes.
Apparently her aunt called them blue, while her uncle said they
were brown. She advanced her face close to me and awaited my
decision.

It is a cruel world. She is an orphan. Her uncle beats her, and
she has no money, and nobody to understand her. The poor
thing broke down and sobbed against me. I did what I could, but
I saw Mrs Varper watching from behind a funnel, and dreaded
her tongue. It was awkward. This ill-treated girl then begged me
to talk with her on some other occasion if I could spare the time.
I said I would. Later that night, as I passed along the deck looking
for the stairs to my cabin, I saw her still standing in the moonlight, close to a young man. He tells me today that she asked him
what colour her eyes were. You see, even details like that worry
her, poor thing. He told her he was a bankrupt, and on his way to
a relation in New York, and she suddenly left his side. It's all very
mysterious, isn't it?

Yours truly,
O. THAKE

We had a dance on board last night, a fancy-dress affair, which was great fun. I was not sure whether to go as a Viking or as a pierrot. Finally I decided on the pierrot as being less trouble and also an easier costume to dance in. Some of the costumes were most picturesque. Mrs Varper came as a Dutch girl, and my moonlight friend, whose name, curiously enough, is Thimbles, as an Irish colleen. With the latter I had several dances. Once during a waltz a ray of light shot at us and illuminated her face. At first I thought someone was tampering with our searchlights. "Shipwreck," I thought. "How dreadful!" But it was only the band's joke. A lot of streamers were distributed, but one cannot be sure of one's aim. I threw one at Mrs Varper, which, unfortunately, did not uncurl, and struck her solidly on the ear.

I noticed several young couples sitting about idly in corners, and not joining in the revelry. It occurred to me that perhaps they did not altogether enjoy these modern dances. So I did my best to organize a set of lancers. Poor things, they did not like to show their appreciation of this, for fear of appearing discourteous to the majority. In fact, I had great difficulty in getting them to take up their positions. The band obliged, and I was about to announce a Sir Roger de Coverley, when, without any warning, the saxophones drowned my voice, and I was too late. The young couples went back to their corners.

Yours truly,
O. THAKE

16

A Mr Campbell has introduced me to the captain, who seems a very nice man. He, the captain, was kind enough to show me a great deal of the ship yesterday, and to explain many technicalities. While we were in his room he showed me various charts and maps and compasses. He told me the depth of the water, but I forget how many yards deep it was, and he explained how he regulates the number of knots per hour. He communicates with almost every part of the ship, though, of course, the actual steering and managing of the engines is done by subordinates, of whom there are a great number. The charts are most elaborate. I gather that we are within several degrees of shoals at the moment, and that the thing is to avoid a reef by keeping to the left of the wind. No, I'm wrong. He says there are no reefs or shoals near us. I was looking at the wrong chart.

I looked through his glasses. "See any land?" he asked, good-humouredly. "No, Captain," I answered, for I think he was chaffing, "No land, but lots of sea," I added. And we joined in the laugh that followed. He then said we were in for a storm. I asked him how he could tell, and he pointed out the white tops of the waves, heavy clouds ahead of us, and a terrific hurricane that blew one's hat off if one removed one's hand from one's hat-guard. "I believe you are right," I said to him, and he agreed.

Yours ever,
O. THAKE

P.S. Tell Saunders to send out a luminous prismatic compass.

Since I last wrote the wind has increased in violence, and the waves have become larger and more frequent. The storm is upon us with full fury. The deck slants first up, then down, so that it is difficult to write in such circumstances. I am told that the thing to do is to keep the feet up and the ears warm. A lady who is on her way to visit her eldest daughter in New York has very kindly given me some of her Zappo. She says it prevents seasickness . . .

It doesn't seem very good stuff. Perhaps a brandy and soda . . .

I feel better and the lady has given me some dry biscuits. The captain has sent a sailor to ask if I would like to see over the engine room. I said I would like to very much later on . . .

A sailor has brought me some tobacco from an officer. I promised to try it yesterday. Really – one does not wish to appear discourteous . . . I put it in my pocket and told the sailor to tell the officer it was very nice. Rather hypocritical, but . . .

I must go and lie down. It is so uncomfortable with the boat going up and down so much. Another lady has offered me some Goppo. I'm afraid I was rather curt, but I don't put much faith in these patent remedies. People are most kind, but one's nerves get rather frayed. Someone has just handed me some Bippo. I really think I shall go and lie down for a little while. I will finish this letter later, if I feel better.

Yours ever,
O. THAKE

P.S. Tell Saunders to send out my Old Etonian braces.

You will not hear from me for a few days, as I shall be occupied with the bustle and hustle of my arrival. The captain says we may sight land at any moment. It is a great adventure. I feel like Columbus, and I'm trying to collect my luggage at the moment. My hat-guard burst during the storm, and I lost the hat overboard, but naturally one does not stop a ship of this magnitude to recover a hat. Besides I have others with me. They say reporters come on board before we land. Mrs Varper has already written up her name for them to put in their papers as "among recent arrivals from Berkhampstead". She says she is very thrilled.

Someone has just shouted "Land!" I thought they always added a "Ho!" But after all, steam changed old customs, and — they are all rushing up to the railings. I must wind up.

Yours ever,
O. THAKE

P.S. Tell Saunders I'm told I may need my goloshes if I go to Palm Beach.

❖ III ❖

AMERICA

My Dear Beachcomber,

Here, as you see, I am. I am staying in a big hotel, and hasten to write to you. I know you will be interested in my impressions. Well, yesterday I went out to take a look at things. I was going along what they call Fifth Avenue, when who should I run into but Tom Watson. Just fancy! He is over here on some business matter. Apparently his mother was to have come with him, but there was some hitch at the last moment. One of his sisters developed quinsy quite suddenly. A doctor was summoned, and would not hear of Mrs Watson sailing, after being exposed to the infection. So there was nothing for it but for Tom to come by himself.

Tom, by the way, has bought the house he was after – you know the one near Dorchester. He hadn't even time to see that the drains were all right before sailing, but he gives me to understand that his brother-in-law (Harvey) has seen to it. Effie is to be a bridesmaid at the Simpson wedding. Won't it be splendid? Dear, dear, I am chattering on like Lord Tennyson's brook, but really it is so delightful to see a face one knows so far from home. And Tom of all people! I must wind up before I use all the hotel paper!

Yours ever,
O. Thake

P.S. Tell Saunders to send out some of the new ragtimes. The people here love them.

America grows on one. I am already used to being called BO, that being, I imagine, the American diminutive of the word Thake. This morning I astonished Tom Watson by calling him pard, but he took the joke well, and retorted by calling me the cat's moustache, and telling me to "place it there". I went to have a look at the so-called Broadway, and was astonished to see English shaving-brushes in the shop windows. There are also English papers, but naturally, as you will guess, they are some days behind the actual date of the moment. Perhaps I can put it better by saying that the news I read today in the *Daily Express* of some days ago, is the news you read in the same paper of that same date, only some days ago. I mean you actually read it some days ago, although to people out here it was – or rather is – today's, not in actual date, but allowing for transit.

Broadway has a lot of tall buildings. I've seen it all, from the big theatres to the busy wharves. The most imposing sight is the Woolworth building, of which, of course, there are many branches in England. Only this, the mother-building, is, as it were, far larger and much more expensive. I know this to my cost, as I made a few purchases near by for a Miss Scales – (I hasten to explain that she is well over sixty, and deaf). I am trying to chew gum, but do not like it very much yet. I was horrified to see, in a poor quarter, a notice in large letters saying "Hot Dog". This seems to me worse than the French with their snails and frogs.

Yours ever,
O . THAKE

P.S. Tell Saunders to send out my Longfellow. One must get atmosphere.

I am still exploring. I am looking for what a young girl called the "High Spots". When she talked about "hitting" them, I thought she was referring to a shooting gallery, but the Americans use "hit" without meaning violence or marksmanship. I suppose the "High Spots" are places of vantage where you get a good view. I have been to several movies and have seen the same stars as we have in England. Yesterday I went to a musical party. I asked a charming young lady to play "Everybody's Doing It". She did not know it, but said her mother might remember it. Tom Watson was there, and one of the guests called him the canary's hips. He was not very pleased, as you know he is vain of his figure. Do you remember the day when the Pimsgrove girls teased him so – at Chertsey, wasn't it? Or was it Abinger? One of the two, I think.

They asked Tom to sing, and he gave them "Glorious Devon". Someone asked me if I had seen any of Valentino's pictures. Guessing my questioner to be an artistic man, I admitted that I knew little of the old Italian Masters. He then said "I mean Rudolph," and I answered smilingly, "Oh, 'La Boheme'!" They all seemed surprised that a mere Englishman should have any literary or artistic knowledge. I got rather proud after that, and described the Albert Memorial and other monuments in London. I ended by becoming firm friends with a man who winked good-naturedly, and promised to show me the coat Columbus was wearing when he landed.

Yours ever,
O . THAKE

P.S. Tell Saunders – no, it doesn't matter.

I am staying in a most pleasant house, and am snatching a few moments before dinner to write to you. I was told that my host and hostess were prohibitionists, but they evidently are not. Any amount of drink is served at every meal . . . Cocktails all the time one is dressing. A real kick in them, I can tell you . . . Of course, prohibition is all very well for those who have not the sense to stop drinking before their heads are affected. But for the ordinary sensible man it seems to me ridiculous to try to control him in any way . . . They've just brought two more cocktails – why two at a time I don't know. Saves them trouble, I suppose. Saves them time, I suppose. Where was I? Oh, yes. Tomorrow we went to a bathing party somewhere – I don't care where – and Tom Watson has just come in.

Tom's nerves suffer from this excitement. He's swaying about and can't keep still still. He's laughing stupidly or else it's me – I must be deaf or something, because it sounds as if he's playing a concert concertina. Excuse this chatter, but it is good to hear from fou again from you. Besides, I can't find my spectacles – oh, here they are up on my forehead all the time all the time. Atta spectacles! Shoot, kid! I'm a bit sleepy, so I'll stop, as dinner will be served soon now.

Yours ever and ever,
OSWALD BLETISLOE HATTERSLEY THAKE.

P.S. Tell Saunders to feed Topsopsy, old chap.

I have met here an extremely nice man called Hogwasch. He has travelled widely, and assures me that Dixie, Tennessee and Alabama are real places. I was very much interested, and he asked me about places he had heard so much of – Manchester, Birmingham, Liverpool. I told him they were real places too. I do honestly think the time has come for an understanding between England and America. This Mr Hogwasch, for instance, is full of kindly feeling towards us. I could not but reciprocate it. I felt somehow that I represented England; that I was, as it were, an ambassador (unofficial, of course). And when I thought of my country, so far away across such miles of sea, a lump rose in my throat, and my eyes filled. It was a proud and solemn moment when we clasped hands; Thake and Hogwasch; England and America at one. "Two hearts," as I quoted to him, "with only a single thought". And he capped it with "Two minds beating as one".

I drank to his country at dinner tonight, and he responded. He turned out to be on his way to California. "A man like me," he said, "is never his own master."

I suppose he meant the call of the wild. With great friendliness, he offered me a sample of some patent fertilizers and also a collapsible siphon stand. He said he had plenty more in his bag. I asked him if he had no profession, and he said, "Oh, sure. I'm a drummer." Fancy a drummer being rich enough to travel so much. This must indeed be a music-loving nation.

Yours ever,
O. THAKE

P.S. Tell Saunders to send out my bicycle-clips.

27

A Mrs Hampton, who has a son at school at Worthing, and another (an elder one) at Repton, told me that I ought to see Niagara Falls. So I took the night train to Buffalo (reminds me of Buffalo Bill). All the stewards, that is, the attendants on the train, look like French colonial troops. Of course they are not, as you may readily guess. The sleeping accommodation is rather embarrassing. There are several bunks on either side, with upper and lower berths. It's like sitting in a moving church, and the men come round and make up the pews.

The Falls are incredible. Sheer water, you know, uncontrolled, unrestrained, untrammelled, tumbling down to its destination below in tons and tons, day and night, night and day, without let or hindrance, unceasing, sheets of the stuff. It just goes on falling all the time, never stopping, never resting, never pausing.

On the other side of the Falls is Canada. I took off my hat as I saw it, but it blew away (my hat, I mean). I don't know which side it went down, so I suppose I shall have to write to both Governments – a thing I hesitate to do, as international relations are so easily disturbed nowadays. But a hat is a hat, even at Niagara Falls. I put the matter to a man standing near me, and he said, "Guess you're an Englishman." This rather amazed me, as I had been saying "Attaboy!" aloud with reference to the Falls. Really, Americans are most astute, are they not?

Yours ever,
O . THAKE

P.S. Tell Saunders neither my flask, nor my "Sandford and Merton", nor my goloshes, nor my address book, nor my tie-press, nor my Longfellow, nor my boot-trees have arrived. What is the man up to?

On my way back to New York I met in the smoking-saloon a most agreeable man, who addressed me as Smith. I told him my name was Thake, and we shook hands. He then said he knew my married sister, and offered me a cigar. I took the cigar, and explained that I had no sisters. After he had left me, another man came up and said, "Surely you are Mr Thake?" I said I was, and he said he remembered meeting me in Manchester last year, and that I was just the man for whom he was looking. I said I hadn't been in Manchester for ten years. All this conversation, of course, led to friendly feeling on both sides, and he told me that he had just acquired all the stock of an oil concern, and would be delighted to offer me a thousand shares or more, at less than one-tenth their real value. He said they would soon be worth a fortune. We then went into details, and I learned that he was the head of a company formed to work the famous Coney Island Oil Fields. He showed me a pamphlet written by himself. When he asked if I would like anyone to share my good fortune, seeing I was on a good thing, I took the liberty of giving him your name and address. I am so excited about it all.

Of course oil is the great thing today. You see it's essential in so many walks of life – the sewing-machine, the reading-lamp, bicycles, cricket bats, pewter, wrestling – all these require oil, in greater or smaller quantities, as the case may be. And it is something to feel that I, although merely holding a piece of paper, am part of a great concern that will send its fruits across so many waters. I feel the movement of a vast machine – which, again, brings us back to oil – although I am, I fear, nought but a foreign cog-wheel. I hope that this lucky stroke of mine may make both our fortunes.

I have had indigestion rather badly of late from swallowing a considerable amount of this tiresome chewing-gum.

Yours ever,
O. THAKE

P.S. Tell Saunders that my stamp album, which I *did not* ask him to send out, has arrived. Really it is too bad of him.

CABLEGRAM FROM BEACHCOMBER TO MR THAKE:—

Do not buy for me Coney Island oilfields not very well known have put all my money in Sussex coffee plantation – BEACHCOMBER.

Van Hultinge's Hotel
Swampscott, Mass

I thought I would have a regular American meal, so I went into a restaurant and ordered buckwheat cakes, crullers, hot tamales, and Horsford's Acid Phosphate. I got into conversation with the gentleman next to me, and he told me he was a descendant of the Pilgrim Fathers, and asked me to accompany him to Swampscott, Mass., where I should get a glimpse of small-town life. I accepted his invitation with pleasure. We set off together, after he had told me his name was Hufnagle. I learned as soon as I reached his house that I should meet, that evening, some Daughters of the Revolution. I supposed it was some local movement, but my neighbour at dinner, a Miss Hissing, explained how England's cruelty rankled with them, and how the tax had upset every-body. I did not like to press her for details, but I did not quite follow all this talk about taxes, and she said someone had thrown a lot of tea into a harbour. All very bewildering. However, I certainly understood that England had been very unreasonable. I said as much, and they asked me to address the meeting.

I talked for a bit about revolutions, and how they annoy everybody, and then I said what a nuisance taxes are, and quoted some old lines about tea. I put in a bit about pilgrims and pilgrimages, as a compliment to my host and hostess, and said that I thought it was our duty, theirs particularly, to establish freedom upon a broad base, to reach out to higher ideals and loftier conceptions, and to avoid bloodshed at all costs. "Daughters of the Revolution," I concluded, "our own Gladstone . . ." – but I fear I have forgotten what I said. They seemed very pleased, and gave me a copper medal with a ribbon attached. Under it was written, "Up and On". I shall have it framed and mounted, and put above my desk in Jermyn Street, when I get home.

Yours ever,
O. THAKE

P.S. Tell Saunders to see that Topsy gets plenty of exercise.

Volstead Hotel
New York

That Oil Fields business has not turned out very well. It has, in fact, turned out badly. I am afraid I shall be kept pretty busy for the next few days, so you may not hear from me. I am trying to get a book on American Law. I think I shall take the thing into court.

Now will you please tell Saunders that I am dissatisfied with his conduct of late? You might also find out, if you can, what has gone wrong with him. Why, for instance, should he forward me a Band of Hope leaflet? And why did he send me a tin of biscuits? I am sure I never asked for those things. Tell him also to keep the plants watered. I do so hope the fellow is not going off his head. You might test him with a few straightforward remarks. Of course, he may be in love again. He is a great nuisance at times. I shall never forget the time he was pursuing the baker's daughter. He used to do the most extraordinary things. One day he brought me a leg of mutton on a tray, instead of the letters. Mrs Voyle was there. Most awkward.

Really, troubles never come singly. I arrived here with some English stamps in my case, left over from England. I find I have been putting them on many of my letters, so I suppose they have not arrived. I hope yours escaped this fate. Of course, it's all my fault, I know. Also my collars have begun disappearing one by one. I had to come down in a scarf this morning. Then, to crown all, what do you think arrived from Saunders? A watering-can. Yes, my dear Beachcomber, nothing more or less than a watering-can. What does all this mean? I am most worried.

This bombardment of foolish things is very tiresome. Tell Saunders I am extremely aggrieved.

Yours ever,
O. THAKE

Volstead Hotel
New York

I really begin to think there is some conspiracy against me. It is all most disturbing. This Oil Fields business will drive me crazy. I can't find anything in American Law that deals with such things. Furthermore, the most ridiculous things continue to arrive from Saunders. Yesterday a halma board, and now today an etching of

Norfolk Cathedral which belonged to my grandfather, and arrived with the glass smashed. It isn't the glass one cares about so much, but the whole idea is so silly. Fancy sending such a thing out! It merely makes me a laughing-stock, with such absurdities littered all over my room. Only last night Tom Watson said, "What a good, attentive man you have in Saunders!"

Do please go and see what is the matter with him.

I have bought some collars, but they were all stolen as soon as I brought them home. So were the next lot. And now whoever does it has begun on my shirts. I have informed the police, and also the lift man. And now I've got the jumps. I believe my chambermaid is a detective in disguise, and is trying to prove that I am stealing the things myself. The way she looks at me! Excuse my incoherence. Find out if it is still the baker's daughter – I mean the Saunders business. I wish the man would marry sensibly, and get over these aberrations. Quite by mistake, being nearly distracted, I've cut old Mrs Vellum – you know her brother used to dive from a great height in Cornwall to amuse the kids – not Cornwall, Devon. I cut her, and she has written an angry note. I could not help it, could I? Oh, dear, oh, dear!

Yours ever,
O. THAKE

P.S. Tell Saunders he can have Sunday off – if that will help.

IV

LONDON AND
MRS BARLOW

My Dear Beachcomber,

As you will see from the above address I am back in Jermyn Street once more. My return was rather rapid. The oil business turned out badly, and also I wanted to be back for the Season in London. It seems as though I had been away a long time, and yet it doesn't, if you know what I mean. I found an enormous mass of correspondence awaiting me, including a letter from Mrs Hawkley telling me that the Colonel is in Scotland – no, it was Ireland. I think you met their boys once – darkish hair, and rather tall for twins. One of them, I forget which, either the younger or the elder, is going up to Woolwich (or Sandhurst) and then into the Army. It will be rather nice for him, won't it?

It is good to be home, in a way. It is like coming back to everything. It's hard to express. What I mean is, it's a sort of return to things, don't you think? I always feel like that about it, somehow. Saunders, with all his failings, is most efficient. I find everything in order, even the saucer of milk for Freckles in the sitting-room, by the revolving bookcase; and this morning he brought my tea, and said, "A fine day, sir," just as if nothing had happened. It wasn't – but that's his way. He tells me the Wansgroves have bought a house called Bewick somewhere near some Welsh place, and that the banging in the street is not as bad as it was before I left. That is good news. He has even fed the canary, which looks fatter than ever. Cause and effect; food makes fatness, eh? Upon my soul, that's almost a slogan, what?

Yours ever,
O . THAKE

P.S. It's too bad. I find that all those things I wrote to Saunders for, from America went out there after I had left for home. I must write and get them back, if I can remember what they were.

*380a Jermyn Street
London, W—*

I am settling down again. I find a number of invitations awaiting me, including one from a Mrs Thallett, a relative, I believe, of the Thallett who invented electric harpoons. You know, there's nothing like London. It's so *big*. It's somehow built on a grand scale – so many buildings and people, more than anywhere else. I suppose I'm what the world calls a Londoner – at heart. I love the bustle and the crowds. I shall never forget Mrs Fume saying to me once, "London, my dear Mr Thake, is England in miniature." Well, if you think that out, you will find it is true. And again, London is, after all, the very heart of our great Empire, with its dominions, protectorates and dependencies. One blood, one flag. One hates to boast, but really, I think we are "It" as young Pollington always says. (Not Edgar, his brother.) You remember he was one of the first to wear Oxford trousers, which I really could never understand. I think the best thing said about them was by Lady Flogge. She said, "The further, the broader." Good, eh? She is a most witty woman, and her collection of third century amber is most remarkable. I am dining with her on Tuesday – next Tuesday, I mean. Which reminds me, will you come and dine one day next week? We have much to discuss, and I will show you some photographs taken during my travels. I must end now, as I am expecting old Thistle any minute. Such a nice man, but obstinate.

By the way, a soup tureen has arrived from America. Saunders knows nothing about it.

Yours ever,
O. THAKE

*380a Jermyn Street
London, W—*

I was at the opera the other night, and I must say the German atmosphere surprised and rather disgusted me. I had no idea they were going to sing in German. Of course, one is prepared to make allowances – I mean, one is ready to forgive them their music – (not that it isn't beautiful music) – but I do think it should be conducted and sung in the mother tongue. With representatives from all quarters of our vast Empire constantly visiting here, it is surely important to create a good impression among the English-speaking races. One South African I know quite well expressed his surprise at the German singing. Let us forgive and forget, by all means, let bygones be bygones, but let us keep that sense of proportion which is, as Gladstone well recognised, one of our most valuable assets.

If people cannot be found to translate the German, could it not be sung in Italian or Belgian or French? This, I am certain, would bring us and our allies nearer together, and produce a feeling of mutual esteem and love. Not only would it be a compliment, but it would avoid giving offence to the millions comprising this great British Empire. Besides, the German language is not as beautiful as others, and "Tristram and Iseult", for instance, would be far more intelligible, at any rate, in England, if sung in English. I feel confident that I am voicing the opinion of the vast majority of Britishers in this matter. Tom Watson is writing a letter to the Press about it.

Yours ever,
O. THAKE

P.S. In any case, why not play "Pinafore" or "The Gondoliers" at Covent Garden? Is English opera dead?

380a Jermyn Street
London, W—

What a relief an English dinner-party is after foreign ones! Foreigners, like all commercial-minded people, talk of politics and religion and other serious things. It is such a strain. Last night I was at the Bunnards' – Cecil Bunnard, you know, the collector. We had a most enjoyable evening. Lady Porringer was there with Myrtle, and old Fenchurch, still grousing, and Mabel Weald and Dr Flaring. I sat next to Barbara Bagge. She tells me her Sealyham has got synovitis, but she has built one of the new hygienic kennels for it, and hopes for the best. I asked the doctor what he thought of it, and he said that disease in men and animals varies considerably. Old Fenchurch said that it was a disgrace that medical science was powerless against mange. Bunnard retorted, "It depends what you call mange." Then a bishop said with a laugh, "It depends what you call medical science." The talk then turned on Tony Monteith's will. Somebody said he had left a lot to his dentist.

Mabel Weald said how brave it was of men to swim in the Serpentine in this weather, and Flaring pooh-poohed the suggestion that cold water cured liver complaints. He then told a long story about a man who had never been cured after years of cold water. After which some one remarked on the trouble the Horse Guards must take to keep spotless.

After we joined the ladies, Mrs Bunnard's niece played a piece of Rachmaninoff, called, I think, "Prologue", and, as an encore, Hoffmann's "Barcarolle". Her touch is very good indeed. Lady Porringer has asked me to dinner next week, to meet Witham, the inventor.

The "Sandford and Merton" I asked Saunders for, and which he sent too late, has just returned from America. Unfortunately Saunders returned it again, without consulting me, so I must get it back again.

Yours ever,
O.THAKE

380a Jermyn Street
London, W—

It was with feelings of some surprise (excuse this scrawl, but Freckles is perched on my shoulder, and is mewing) that I read your last letter about the young woman who wishes to meet me. I suppose I am rather out of date in my notions of propriety – but really! It takes my breath away. You withhold, quite rightly, her name, and I cannot think who she can be. It could not – no it could not be that Miss Paddell I met at the Corringtons'. Really you will think me vain, but Tom Watson told me she was evidently trying to vampire me, as the Americans say. She asked me for my photograph, but I am sure she intended to stop at that. Besides, I know her brother in the Navy. Could it be the Fidge girl? Surely not. Of course I am merely speculating. I would not for worlds pursue the matter in these days. Paula-Hicks-Gobble? The widow? Don't tell me that! But wait! It is clearly some one I have never met, as she desires, you say, to be introduced to me. I had forgotten that. It's no good my puzzling any more.

Did you see Lady P ___ 's portrait in the "Gabbler" last week? I was at the theatre with her the other night. I forget what it was called, but the jokes – well, I hope none of the women present understood them. I fear they did, as Constantia P ___ , who sat beside me, kept nudging me and saying, "Do you see the point? Did you get that?" Of course she only wanted me to explain the jokes, so I said, sternly, I fear, "No, I do not get any of them. Dull, I assure you." She winked, and her mother rebuked her. Rather awkward, what? To appease the girl, I delved into my play-going memories, and told her one or two lines from "Little Lord Fauntleroy" and "East Lynne". She said she preferred "Piff-Poff" and her mother again rebuked her. A dear, good woman, Lady P ___ .

Saunders will drive me mad. He has now returned to America the stamp album that was returned from there to me here, after he had sent it there. What is one to do?

Yours ever,
O. THAKE

*380a Jermyn Street
London, W—*

If there is one thing I like about the Academy, it is the, as it were, social aspect of it. One meets everybody there, and it isn't necessary to be a highbrow to go there. I mean they are not all experts, and they don't talk all the time about the technique of the pictures. In fact, many people I know keep off the subject of painting altogether, and treat the occasion as purely social, which is rather a relief. The Relfs are like that. To meet them, you'd never think they'd know a good picture from a bad one, or vice versa. Yet he, I believe, once studied art, and she has written a guide to the Prado in Madrid.

I struck a good day at the Academy, and bumped into a lot of friends. We all went round together – "as if it was golf" as Percy said. Though I pointed out that we were too many for golf.

There was some trouble over Mrs Bowley. She is so short sighted, and would insist on reading out from the catalogue. Of course, she confused portraits with cabbage, and generals with bridges, and so on. There was much laughter, but old age will be served. And anyhow, one can generally tell roughly what a picture is meant to be.

There are not enough seats, I think. It is so inconvenient to have to carry on a conversation standing up. But, on the whole, it was a good show, except that the Pargetters were away in Hampshire. They are usually the life and soul of such occasions. However, we laughed a lot, and swapped holiday news. I enclose a snapshot of myself taken by Myrtle in the Sculpture Room. It was signed by her brother, in a playful moment.

Yours ever,
O. THAKE

380a Jermyn Street
London, W—

I had tea at Colonel Farley's yesterday, and played my first tennis of the season. I think one's first game is somehow different from the rest, don't you? I suppose the reason is simply that it is the first game – I mean, one is out of practice more than afterwards, and consequently cannot get the grip of things. After, of course, it is different. I played with Miss Paxted – you remember her cousin, who wrote the novel called "Dripping" – well, she (I mean that cousin) is some sort of a relation of Maude Farley's. I got one or two good shots in, but Sybil Paxted will run after the balls between strokes which is most irritating. We played the Pink-water girl and her brother, and beat them as far as we got. It was too dark to finish. Pinkwater told me a good budget story, which I forget. You know what a wag he is.

During tea Cyril Blankett arrived. He's got some new idea about planting delphiniums, all rather technical. The Colonel collared him and told him to try it on the pansies. Cyril was furious, and pointed out, half in fun, that a delphinium and a pansy are very different affairs. "Both flowers," snorted the Colonel. It was most amusing. Maude Farley can't stand Cyril. I think it's his red moustache. You never know, do you? As I was helping to roll up the net, the rain began. So we were just in time. By the way, do you remember Olive Watts? Well, she didn't go to Finland after all. She may later, according to Molly. But you know Molly!

Yours truly,
O. THAKE

The Towers
Westborough

I am at the Towers, as you will notice, for the week-end. Today being Sunday, we are all more or less doing nothing. Madge is here, and is reading rather a good leader from one of the Sunday papers. There will be church later on, and young Effington is to read the lessons. After that we shall probably chat with Sopwith, the vicar. Then home to lunch. In the afternoon – I don't quite know. We are divided. My host and hostess rather want to sleep.

Some of the rest of us suggest going on the lawn to read, while others favour a walk to the Arnolds' next door, to hear about Walter Arnold's new car. One way, of course, and I have suggested as much, would be to send a note by one of the maids to the Arnolds asking them round. Which course will be adopted one can hardly say as yet. I do not much care myself. Anyhow, I've half promised to go and see Tony's rabbits.

Later.

It rained after lunch, so I suggested a rubber. To my surprise, our host said that he loathed playing bridge in the rain. He said bridge was depressing enough without that. Madge then suggested the gramophone, but no one could find a needle. I offered to give them my talk on America, the one that I gave at the Wilmingtons' garden party, but it appears that our host loathes Americans. Fortunately it stopped raining, and we were able to go to call on the Arnolds. They were out. You will remember that Arnold and I were at Oxford the same time as Tom Watson. By that time it was raining hard again, and we returned. Our host had gone to sleep by the fire, so I read the life of Charles Dickens until tea. A remarkable man.

Later.

Madge says she will drop in on you on her return. She is motoring home early on account of the serious illness of her aunt. When I asked the name of her aunt, she said "Banbury", but I know no one of that name. Perhaps her aunt has married since then, however.

Yours ever,
O. THAKE

380a Jermyn Street
London, W—

Each year the Glorious Fourth of June finds me a little older, a little further on the way to old age, a little further, too, from youth. But what a fine thing it is to go back to one's old school, to the buildings and fields one knew so well. All the faces, of course, are different, since those who were boys with us are boys no longer, but men, according to the inexorable decrees of fate. Yet these boys of today are boys like us – that is, as we used to be before we became men. And who can hear the old school songs without choking? They are like nothing on earth to one who revisits the scenes of his boyhood. Then again, it is so fine to see the thing going on like a tree. Boys leave, but other boys take their places. Thus the thing goes on. Dear me, I am becoming quite sentimental.

I met a bishop I knew, a former schoolmate of mine, and he chaffed me about my inky fingers, and I reminded him that he used to say "damn" when his shins were kicked. He laughingly denied this, but all in the best-humoured way. He was not at all offended, which is proof that the Church is broader-minded than some people seem to think. Lady ___ was there. One of her boys is quite a swell – Pop, and all that. As long as England can breed this kind of stuff nobody need fear for the future of our Empire. I tell you what's wrong with France. *She's got no Eton*. A Fourth of June would do her no end of good and stop all the nonsense. I'd like to see the Wall Game in their dreadful Latin Quarter. You, as a writer, ought to be able to get an article out of this idea.

Well, another Fourth is over, and here I am again. Floreat Etona! Yes, indeed!

Yours ever,
O. THAKE

P.S. Tom, of course, to the everlasting regret of his family, went to Harrow – good in its way, of course – but – well – you know.

380a Jermyn Street
London, W—

I have been taking advantage of the fine weather. Yesterday I went down to Marlham, where the Wraglans have a house. They got up a party to go out in their new launch, Moonbeam. But, as we were rather a large party, we split up. I was asked to take Mrs Barlow in one of the punts. Her husband, who died in Sweden, was something to do with structural anatomy. She spoke continually of his medals. She is a nice woman, and tactful. My punting is a little stale, and I think she saw this, as she kept on suggesting that we should go down a quiet backwater, where there would be no people. I was too proud to take the hint at first, but after one or two knocks, and after getting the pole stuck, I gave in. I said to her, "This is no time for *amour propre*." She only winked, which may have been to disguise the fact that she has no sense of humour. "*Amour*," she said, "but why drag in the *propre?*" As you see, she has not much conversation, and what there is is a little stupid.

Eventually I got the boat into a backwater, and she suddenly said her hands were cold, and asked me to feel them. Of course, it was all her imagination. They were quite warm. Really, women do fidget and fuss so. I was just going to sit down and rest at the end of the boat, when she said there was a moth or something in her eye. I went over to examine the eye, but could see nothing there. Very soon after this, she said she was going to faint. I propped her up on cushions, and splashed some water on her. She kept saying, "Hold me, hold me. I'm falling." I said, "You

47

can't fall. You are sitting down." Then she got angry, and asked to be taken home. What can one do? I can't make anything of women. They are extraordinary creatures.

Dilke has gone to Pevensey.

Yours ever,
O. THAKE

P.S. Tom Watson says perhaps she is what the young people call a river girl.

Senior Constitutional Club
Pall Mall, London W—

This is surely the weather for your name – I believe beachcombers have a pretty cool time of it. Anyhow they ought to, if they are always by the sea. But really the heat is terrific, is it not? I only remember one month as hot – somewhere back in '99, I think – or was it '98? It was the year old Lady Shamburn's boy went into the Navy. I know that, because his cousin and I used to meet at their uncle's place. How keen the old lady was on her greenhouses. But come, come! Fancy talking about greenhouses in this heat. Green-land (!) would be more appropriate, would it not? I mustn't ramble, but it is so hard to concentrate. One's brain seems to melt. I wonder if there will be a drought. It is so rough on the farmers when there is no water about – and how the cattle live is a mystery. Who would be a cow in this weather? Not I! Nor you, I am sure, eh? I am staying at my club until the heat wave passes.

I have had a letter from Mrs Barlow. She says the river is the only cool place, and will I take her out one evening in a punt again. I don't quite know how to reply. She is so fussy, but I mustn't offend her, as, after all, she is a friend of very good friends of mine – and of my friends too. Besides, it is so difficult to get away from the crowds – please do not misunderstand me. My doctor has a theory that punting, by opening the pores, is good in this weather. But I should have thought that applied equally to other forms of exercise, wouldn't you? Don't trouble to answer till it's cool. He may mean it does. He says it doesn't, at any rate.

I was wrong about Dilke. He is at Marsfield.

Yours ever,
O . T H A K E

P.S. Tell Saunders to keep the wine near open windows.

Wellington House
Esher

I am in somewhat of a muddle. Owing to the carelessness of Saunders – really, he grows too provoking – I have been consulting last year's diary instead of this year's. The result is, that acting on last year's entries, I arrived the other night at the Farringtons' at Maidenhead, expecting to go to Ascot with them. They, of course, were not expecting me, and there were some awkward moments. I produced my diary triumphantly, and Olga cried, "Why, it's 1927." This I flatly denied, and fetched a newspaper to prove my point. "I mean the diary," she said. Sure enough, when I looked at the diary, it said 1927. They put me up, but I felt most uncomfortable. Next day, I sent for the 1928 diary, and proceeded, according to the entries, to the Stoddarts at Windsor, only to discover that Saunders had sent the 1926 diary. At last I got the right book, and am where I ought to be – at Esher, with the Dewsworthys.

Last night, over the port, we had a long discussion on Nicaragua. When we joined the ladies, I was surprised to see Mrs Barlow at the piano. She asked me to turn over for her. I told her I couldn't read music, but the only reply she made was, "I wonder if we can go on the river here." I said I did not think one could, and began to talk of Ascot. "I hope you will win the Gold Cup, Mr Thake," she said. I felt rather stupid – she does say unexpected things. She then asked me if I thought Green suited her. I said I did not know the gentleman, thinking she meant to marry again. She replied, "I mean the colour."

Well, what can one say to such a woman? Really, she is beyond me.

Yours ever,
O . T H A K E

Wellington House
Esher

There's something about a London season – a sort of something – I can't describe it, but you know what I mean. One is conscious of things happening, and one meets people and goes to places. I must say I should miss my Ascot if ever the Socialist people abolished it. It is a sort of landmark, and you know where you are, if you know what I mean. I don't see what one could put in its place. I was with the Dewsworthy party yesterday. Her father was Canon – oh, I forget his name – anyhow, he was a Canon, and so, of course, they are all very much against betting. But as Pearl, the eldest daughter says, after all, one needn't bet if one goes to Ascot.

I met Tom Watson in the paddock, and he introduced me to a jockey, rather a small man. "May the best horse win," I said to him. "Not if I know it," he answered. So I said, "Well, anyhow, I sincerely hope you do know it." At which we both laughed. I asked him whether he found it tiring to ride so much, and he said, in the most natural way, "Oh, no." He then told me a wonderful story about some horse or other, but Mrs Barlow was at my elbow, and I missed half of it. She said she "was very fond of horses, as her husband used to ride one frequently". She asked me if I liked chestnut roans, and I said I did, without thinking. Of course, I don't. She then made me explain everything to her – race cards and so on. And then she got on the river again, and asked me to take her to Henley. I rather hesitated, as I'm taking my nephew, Parkstone, and she may set her cap at him. One never knows, does one?

Tell Saunders not to send on any more circulars. It makes one look so silly, when one is in some one else's house.

Yours ever,
O. THAKE

Wellington House
Esher

Yesterday was marred for me by certain embarrassing situations. Really, Mrs Barlow is the most extraordinary woman. She led me away into the paddock, and while I was holding her sunshade and her vanity-bag, she took her mirror, and, dabbing her nose, approached close to me, and asked if she looked all right. At that very unfortunate moment, up came Tom Watson and his crowd. I hurriedly told her that her hat was a little crooked, and she appeared to become angry. Tom looked curiously at us, and passed on. She then took my arm, and said she hadn't meant to be nasty, and I could call her Ethel if I liked. Really! I should have her calling me Oswald! It's all very disturbing. One does not know what to do for the best.

Yours affectionately,
O. THAKE

P.S. Can you do nothing to stop Saunders sending on these preposterous circulars? Two or three of the party have noticed, and it places me in an absurd situation.

36 Disraeli Crescent
Kensington
London W—

DEAR MR BEACHCOMBER,

Your bad taste in publishing to the world the letters that Mr Thake thinks it fit to write to you has reached a point where I must protest. He continually couples my name with his own, and even hints that I am, as it were, pursuing him. I assure you that nothing but his colossal vanity is responsible for this delusion. Like all men, he thinks himself irresistible. By bad fortune we have been thrown together a good deal lately, and although I should be the last to deny the brilliance of his conversation and the power of his personality, the whole thing is most annoying, as my brother's son, who is at Harrow, has already been asked by his comrades who this Mr Thake is, and whether he is a good friend of mine.

If you must continue to publish the correspondence of this vain man, might I request that you exercise a little censorship to spare my feelings? The scene he described in the paddock is too ludicrous for words. I may have asked if I looked all right, but all women do that. As for my proximity to him, it was due to the crush.

Yours truly,
ETHEL HUMMING-BARLOW (O.B.E.)

In deference to the feelings of Mrs Barlow, whose letter I have published above, I have endeavoured to censor anything in the following letter from Mr Thake which might cause any offence to her susceptibilities. I hope I have succeeded, without, at the same time, marring my friend's correspondence.

Wellington House
Esher

DEAR BEACHCOMBER,

I always seem to be complaining, but really one thing happens after another. I have read Mrs ___ 's letter to you, and can only say it leaves me amazed and more convinced than ever of the incomprehensibility of women. Some one called them sphinxes. It is true. They are. Mrs ___ omits to say that it was she who . . . and . . . so, you see, her letter gives a false impression. As for the paddock scene, I repeat that she shamelessly followed . . . I couldn't get away from . . . try as I might, and indeed, did. With . . . aforethought, she not only . . . but . . . so I leave you to judge. Besides, what can I do? I can't refuse to meet her, and she turns up everywhere I go. Clearly . . . Don't you see? I don't, for a moment suggest that she wants to marry . . . but . . .

Yesterday was again spoiled for me. Mrs ___ made me carry her sunshade, and we lost the Dewsworthy car, and had to go back together in a hired one. She held . . . hand. What could I do? Really, the thing is beyond a joke. Thank goodness, Ascot is over. I feel I want a rest cure after the attentions of this . . . lady . . .

Yours ever,
O . THAKE

P.S. On no account must Saunders discuss this . . . with cook. It has gone too . . . already.

380a Jermyn Street
London, W—

I looked in at a large garden party yesterday. It was most entertaining. I was surrounded by a number of delightful young ladies, who sold me any number of tickets. Of course, I had not met any of them before, but the free and easy ways of the young nowadays are a proverb. Besides, I don't think there is anything *really* wrong, when the intentions are good. One cannot always be introduced, after all. My tickets turned out to be for fortune-tellers, and I had a busy time of it. The first told me I should have ten children. I laughed it off, and moved on to the second who said I was fond of animals, and ought to marry a fair-haired woman. The third said I should go on a journey and receive a letter. (I wonder what journey it can be? I had not thought of one). The fourth told me I should marry a dark widow and inherit a fortune, and have an illness at sixty-eight.

I had tea in a tent with a lot of people, and somebody asked me to enter for a horse-race. I excused myself, as I had no riding clothes with me. They all laughed at that, so I said, "Anyway, the hat is all right, whatever the rest is." One girl, an actress, wanted to get back to her theatre in a hurry, and wondered if she could get a taxicab. I said I thought she could. She said she hated going alone, so I introduced her to another girl I had met earlier in the afternoon.

Yours ever,
O . THAKE

P.S. I saw Mrs ___ with poor Tom Watson today. He was apparently trying to get a fly or something out of her eye.

❧ V ❧

THE EPISODE OF
THE BASSOON

My Dear Beachcomber,

Things are really going too far. Yesterday the newspapers published a photograph of me, alleged to be taken at the Theatrical Garden Party, in what, as far as I can judge, was a *yachting cap* (or was it a porter's? – no, it couldn't be, because I haven't one). You will agree that it makes me look absurd. What man of my standing would go dressed in this imbecile manner? It hints that I don't know better than to discard the top hat, which is the *sine qua non* at social functions. I would as soon think of going to a dance in my college blazer. What my friends are thinking, I can only guess from continual telephone calls, and a telegram from Tom Watson saying 'What's the Chelsea crossing like?' Well, what can I reply? I'm not sure my best course will not be to say that I was acting a yachtsman in one of the side-shows. But then, everyone knows I don't act. You see what a position I am in. Fun is fun, and I hope I am not lacking in a sense of humour, but there's a limit.

An American lady whom I met recently has asked me to play a bassoon in a jazz band at one of her charity shows. I don't know what I can have said to lead her to suppose I am a musician. She is an agreeable woman, and one hates to disappoint, but one's duty does not include bassoon playing – at least, not that I ever heard of – and on top of this photograph too – it's like living in a nightmare. What with Lady H— asking if I had spent the afternoon in the boot-leggers' tent, and Sybil chaffing me about ropes and spars and sails – I don't know which way to turn. And why a bassoon more than any other instrument? Jazz, indeed! May things straighten out is the prayer of

Yours ever,
O.THAKE

P.S. Tell Saunders I said it doesn't matter, and it doesn't.

*380a Jermyn Street
London, W—*

I wonder who it was who said, "Man is like a spark, because he is bound to get into trouble." How true! I am being pestered to death over this ridiculous concert. The American lady who is giving the charity show will not believe me when I tell her I can't play the bassoon for her. She says it is my modesty. And now she has sent me a lot of music, with the bassoon parts in red ink, for me to practise before the first rehearsal. She even called the other day, and insisted on going over the score with me. How can I remember all this impossible nonsense? She made me look at something called "I Gotta Gal," and told me how to emphasize special notes and all that. I said, "My dear lady, this is all Greek to me." "With your education," she said, "you sure know Greek." And she turned to another piece of music, on which was written, "Why Can't You Kiss Me Like The Baby Next Door?" which she said was an encore for the "Railway Blues". How unintelligible all this is! And when I said I couldn't produce any bassoon she said I was shy, and hunted all over the room for it.

Bassoon! I ask you! What am I to do? She won't believe me, and when she asked Saunders, "I suppose your master often plays to himself?" the fool shuffled and said, "Yes, madam. Certainly, madam." I frowned at him, but she saw me, and said again,

"How modest you are. I'd like to get a reporter on to you."
Heavens! Supposing she does! She's capable of anything. I have
told Saunders to say, if any reporter calls, that I'm at St Raphael.
The thing is too terrible. My aunt has heard about it, and came
and lectured me for mixing myself up in "vulgar theatricals" as
she calls them. "A violin," said she, "I could understand, but a
bassoon! Ugh! A music-hall instrument, my dear Oswald. I
suppose you know that in these vulgar bands the players shout
American words."

Was ever such a tangle of misunderstanding?

Yours truly,
O . T H A K E

*380a Jermyn Street
London, W—*

I thought it was all over, but it isn't. A terrible individual called
on me yesterday. He said he was the conductor of the Jazz band
the American lady was getting together. He said he had known
the lady, Mrs Mawgrie, in Xenophon, and that she always put
pepper into things. I asked if she had been a cook, and he
laughed, and said "No." Then he launched out into a lot of
jargon about the music we were going to play. He kept saying,
"It's Noise that gets 'em." I couldn't get a word in, and I was
afraid someone would call, and hear him shouting all this stuff at
me. But he gave me a chance when he asked how I proposed to
do the porter's yell in the "Dixon-Mason Line" chorus. I said, "I
do not propose to do it at all. Further, I do not propose to mix
myself up in this preposterous affair. Here is my cheque for the
charity, but I have never played the fool like this, and never will.
You may tell Mrs Mawgrie that my decision is final."

The only reply I have had from Mrs Mawgrie is a note thanking me for my cheque, and telling me that I am expected at the first rehearsal. Is everybody mad? Do I look like a bassoon player? What is there about me that singles me out for all this nightmare of nonsense? Or is it somebody's practical joke? Try to imagine, if you can, a man in my station of life being asked by a noisy man, very much overdressed, how he proposes "to do the porter's yell". It is beyond a joke, is it not?

Yours ever,
O. THAKE

380a Jermyn Street
London, W—

I am sure you will be glad to hear that I am at last free of this ridiculous business. I went to the hall where the rehearsal was being held. It was crowded with Mrs Mawgrie's friends. To my surprise, Tom Watson was there, and as I made my way to the front, he said, "Surely you are not going to play?" I merely gave him a look. The horrible young man who had called on me, showed me to a seat on the platform, and handed me a bassoon. I at once blew down it, and produced a startling row. Mrs Mawgrie, in the front row, leaned over, and begged me not to jest. The young conductor told me I was holding my instrument wrong. "Perhaps," I said loudly, but with restraint, "you will now believe that I know nothing of this nonsense." I then blew down it again, and twiddled things with my fingers, until they begged me to desist, as I was demoralising the rest of the orchestra, who, indeed, could scarcely restrain their laughter. So I won my point, and left the hall with all the dignity I could summon, bowing ironically to the young man, and telling Mrs

Mawgrie that if I could serve her in any other way I should be most happy to do so.

Tom Watson overtook me outside, and informed me with gusto that it was he who had told Mrs Mawgrie I was a bassoon player of some skill. I simply looked at him, and said, "Harrow and Balliol! – and then this kind of thing!" I think my tone shamed him, for he made no reply. I raised my hat and left him.

All the publicity the newspapers gave the wretched bassoon business was really too much for me. I fled from it during the night, without even telling Saunders I was going. I do not want anybody to know where I am, therefore I give you no address. I am seeking rest and quiet here beside the sea. I spend the mornings either listening to the band, or amusing myself on one of the two piers. I hardly dare open a newspaper for fear of encountering my name again, and giving the whole show away by making some guilty movement. Please don't give my photograph to any of your reporter friends.

Unluckily I have run into Miss Sparling, who used to organize school outings or something. I told her I wasn't supposed to be here, and she said "Naughty man!" I do hope she won't say anything silly or indiscreet. I said, "You see, Miss Sparling, I have had to leave town hurriedly, and no one is supposed to know where I have gone." She winked and said, "I quite understand." I hope she does. You see she knows the Griddles and Tom Watson.

I keep imagining that people are staring at me. Perhaps it is only my imagination. Oh, drat! I've just remembered that my name is on my trunk and suitcase – and I signed it in the hotel book? It's too aggravating. It really is too bad.

What shall I do? I wrote some ten or eleven letters on arrival, having bought plain envelopes and paper, and I have just got chaffing replies to five of them, accusing me of eloping and so on. Now, how on earth does anybody know my

address? It's simply horrible. I don't understand it. I think I'm
going out of my mind.

Later.

Two more replies! Is the whole world upside down? Tell
Saunders you don't know where I am and not to send letters.

Yours ever,
O . THAKE

P.S. Tell Saunders when I say check trousers I mean check
trousers.

Hotel Colossal
Brighton

Man, as I have often said before, is bound to meet trouble, as the
sparks do. I ran into Mrs Barlow here, and she was so nice to me,
that I couldn't leave her impromptu. She had a young gentleman
with her, who was very nice to me, and flattered me very much,
and I said I would dine with them both last night. The dinner
was a great success. The sole was excellent. The Chateau Yquem
was beyond reproach. We talked of the British Empire. The
young gentleman said he was all for the natives. I said, "It
depends." He said he didn't agree with interference, and quoted
a poem of Mr Kipling's all about the lesser breeds without the
advantage of the law. He followed this up with "Gunga Din,"
which was most realistic. Mrs Barlow said it only showed how
wrong it was of other people to meddle in our affairs.

After dinner I happened to hear the young man telephoning.
He said, "Mr Thake is enjoying and imbibing the ozone in
comparative seclusion at Brighton." The cat is out of the bag –

and what a cat, my dear friend! I do not, of course, refer to the lady. She could not help it. I could do nothing. Obviously the gentleman is one of those who write about me, and where I am. I was powerless. I gave him a cigar, and he asked me what my favourite colour was. I said light blue, and he smiled, suspecting Eton. "Flor-i-at Etona!" he said, putting an "i" for an "e." But what of it? He meant it kindly. So here I am, in the soup. If you have any influence, I beg of you to stop this.

Yours ever,
O . THAKE

P.S. Tell Saunders there is not a single waistcoat in all the suits he sent.

The following paragraph appeared in the London newspapers, fulfilling my friend's worst fears: —
"Mr Thake is enjoying and imbibing the ozone in the comparative seclusion of Brighton. He hopes to return to London in the near future. His favourite colour is, of course, blue."

Hotel Colossal
Brighton

DEAR BEACHCOMBER,

My mind is made up. Things have come to a head, and I am going right away out of Europe, to cut myself off, and have a rest. You will not hear from me again for some considerable time. What happened was this. I had lunched with Mrs Barlow, and we went for a stroll afterwards on the front at Hove. We were talking as we went along, when suddenly the young gentleman who writes for the papers appeared with a friend. Before I knew what was happening, the friend flashed a camera on us, and pulled the trigger. I was most incensed, and made him promise not to publish it. But the next day, I read in a local paper a paragraph coupling my name with Mrs Barlow's and hinting – well, that we were about to be engaged. It is too dreadful. Do you not think I am wise in going away so quickly?

Good-bye then – at least not that sad word. Let us rather say, with our French allies, *au revoir*. I am not as young as I used to be, and the wear and tear of the season, and all these additional worries have had an adverse effect on my nerves. I shall go to some new place where I can meet nobody, and have no letters to answer. When I return I hope we may pick up the thread of our friendship again.

My regards to you.

Yours ever,
O . THAKE

P.S. I am writing full instructions to Saunders, but as he is so muddle-headed, will you tell him to read them carefully? By the way, ask him why he sent my canary down here – and in the wrong cage, at that.

✦ VI ✦

THIN ICE

388a *Jermyn Street*
London, W—

MY DEAR BEACHCOMBER,

If Mahomet can't go to the mountains − to parody a well-known proverb − the mountains must come to Mahomet. I have had quite a Swiss time at the Boyles'. We went off for the day in the car to a place where there was a sheet of ice, and proceeded to out-Arosa Arosa. One got into it fairly well, although one had not been on the ice, speaking for oneself, for some years. Daisy Hopton and Aimée Boyle put me through my paces. The vicar said, "Ah, Mr Thake, a thorn between two roses!" "Alpine roses, vicar," I corrected, and he laughed and told Mortimer, who said he's put it in his next novel. I suppose these writers get a lot of copy from educated conversation. Is that how you do it yourself? However let us return to our muttons − or rather, our ice. It held well in places, but Daisy nearly went in once at the end of a figure of eight, and I challenged her to do the Charleston on skates.

After twilight, she and I were still skating hard, and I remembered somebody saying that an attractive woman on skates is irresistible. She repeated some verse about a harvest moon, and I told her she ought to be on the stage. Where-upon, she went on reciting for a long, long time, and suggested that we should do the love scene from "Paolo and Francesca". She knew it by heart, which was more than I do, having barely heard of it. I did my best under her prompting, but she said my movements were awkward. I reminded her of the threatened thaw. "We may be on rather thin ice," I said. But she got quite sulky, and said, "Don't you like skating on thin ice? It's like playing with fire." I did not

69

see the connection myself till I got home. It made me blush like a boy. But there!

Yours ever,
O. Thake

P.S. Tell Saunders to send me "Paolo and Francesca," unless the thaw is universal.

380a Jermyn Street
London, W—

Really this snowy weather is very beautiful. Even my barber remarked on it this morning. I took a sharp walk in the Park before lunch, and a curious thing happened. I used to scribble verses when I was younger, but not for years have I tried to do so. Well, I suppose the snow moved me, or the sky or something. Anyhow, when I got to the club I sat down and wrote this poem. I wonder if you could get it published for me? Tom Watson read it and liked it, and he, as you know, got a Wordsworth prize at school. He ragged me a bit and called me Apollo. So I called him Neptune and joked about his small ears. It was all very good-natured. But here's the poem, just as I wrote it, without a comma altered. Judge it for yourself, and if you think it good, do as you will with it. I call it "Thoughts in the Park," as that is really what it amounts to, although, of course, it was written in the club. Poetic licence, what? I haven't troubled to explain that in a foot-note, as it surely should be obvious to any reader. Don't you agree?

THOUGHTS IN THE PARK
BY O. THAKE

As I walked through the park,
   I saw the trees all standing still,
And there was snow underfoot,
   And every mound was like a hill.

The frozen grass was bleak and white,
   And on the railings was rime,
The branches were dark as night,
   I heard Big Ben chime.

Women and men with chilled faces,
   Passed me quickly by,
Of sunshine there were no traces,
   And grey was the December sky.

I felt a peaceful feeling,
   As I walked back to my grub,
I felt all was well with the world,
   As I approached my club.

Snow . . . Snow . . . Snow . . . Snow
   I shall remember today,
When the flowers are among us years from now,
   And I am eighty and grey.

380a Jermyn Street
London, W—

I was overjoyed to see that you succeeded in having my little poem printed, but don't think me ungrateful if I point out that I would have preferred to see more made of it. I don't mean more added to it; I mean I would have like to have seen it printed in larger letters and given more of a send-off, as it were. Surely poetry ought not to be hidden away like that among prose, and printed in letters one usually associates with weather forecasts or donations to charity. After all, prose is prose, and poetry is poetry. I mean prose is all right, but poetry elevates the mind. I would print poetry if I were you, which I am, of course, not, – I merely take a hypothetical case – well, then, were I you – which is impossible – but still, if it were, I would print poetry at the top of the page in old-fashioned writing, and with holly round it at this season.

Don't think me too critical, but I have strong views. I remember an article about it once in a review. By the way, the comma in line three of verse one ought to be a semi-colon, for the sake of the pause. This is quite informal, but if ever the thing goes into an anthology I want justice done to it.

How I dwell on my modest effort! Forgive me. Aimée Boyle has asked me to go skating again if the thaw keeps off. Apparently her sister will be of the party. Oh, and about the poem, I suppose it wouldn't be the thing to publish it in other papers – I mean, perhaps I might use an assumed name to make it all right – a different name for each paper, thus giving the impression of a different contributor. But then I get no kudos, unless I explain it was me in a footnote, would I?

Yours ever,
O . THAKE

P.S. Tell Saunders cook may ask the policeman in for Christmas Eve, but not, say, after eleven. It misleads.

I am to play the part of Lothario Brown in a little play young Pierce, the artist, has written for us. It's to be produced here in Mrs Watson's drawing-room, and I'm busy learning my part – that of, as I read it, a dashing, devil-may-care man of the world. Aimée Boyle, whom I eventually marry – I mean, of course, in the play – is to do Amanda. We had our first rehearsal today, and had to read most of our lines. With confounded ill-luck I found, after a while, that I was reading the fraudulent solicitor's part, and when they told me to kiss Betty Ritchie's hand, I made the action of blotting a will. But it all passed off in laughter, and the solicitor (played by Tom Watson) was chaffed for not seizing my opportunity. One of my lines is spoken to Connie Ratchett, and it says, "Your eyes madden me"; of course it means not with rage, but with a softer emotion, as it were. Well, you know she wears glasses – blue glasses; it makes it awkward, and then I ask her to fly with me to Monte Carlo – no, Venice – I'm forgetting my part already – well, she answers – no, I forget what. One can't know everybody's words. But still.

I find I'm really a dreadful character – in the play I mean. It's lucky it's just fun. Aimée is very good, and acts, Tom says, as though she means every word of it. I think I shall get on well with her – in the play, that is, – not that I don't otherwise, but you know. Today at rehearsal, when she fainted in my arms – in the play, of course – Mrs Watson shouted out, "My dear Oswald, you're positively gauche. Have you never held a woman in your arms?" I said never, and they all laughed. Really! One need not be a scamp and a roué, surely, to play the part. Besides, it's all so embarrassing. I wish I were out of it. The girls – well, women – all insist on informal rehearsals all the time. I get no peace. Tom

73

says it's because I'm a bachelor. I wish he wouldn't mix up acting with real life. Botheration!

Yours truly,
O. THAKE

P.S. Tell Saunders to get me some stuff to make eyebrows inky – I mean, in colour – dark black, that is, of course. Mrs Barlow is playing Poppy, and will call me Buddy. It's so ludicrous.

Woodgift House
Maidstone

We decided to go out and sing carols yesterday, before doing our rehearsal of Pierce's play. We went round to the Lomonds', eight of us, and sang outside their door, disguising ourselves as much as we could. As soon as we began the one about Wenceslaus a maid came and told us to go away. I was worked up to a pitch, and cried, "Where is your Christmas spirit?" and I playfully stood on one foot at her. I suppose I was wrong, but Christmas is Christmas, and only comes once. Anyhow, she disregarded me, and addressed herself to Mrs Watson, who had got caught in Tom's trombone. Finally, Mr Lomond came out, and recognising us, asked us in. "What's the joke?" he asked – he is Scottish by descent. Sylvia, the daughter said, "Oh, dad!" but I stepped into the breach by admiring his picture of the Perth Dye Works. He said it was given to his uncle – or great uncle, I forget which – yes, his uncle – by a man called Taggart or something during the Boer war. He got it from their son. We put him in a good humour later by saying "Nicht wi' Burns" and "Truly Rural". And he sang "The Maid o'Peebles" twice for us.

We are getting into our stride — or rather our parts — in the play, and the beards are expected to arrive tomorrow from the shop they are coming from for us — two of them, one red one for Tom, and a small goat one for the vicar who is playing Polo Jack, the young cowboy subaltern. He ordered his by mistake, as he, of course, doesn't have to wear one. So there will be one over. Tom says he will wear both, which is pure nonsense — just fun, naturally. Anyhow, there will be one over. I suggest sending it to a hospital for Christmas. The trilby they got for me is too small, but Aimée is going to heat it, or something, to enlarge it. I hope it won't shrink again. But if it does, I suppose it could be heated again. Betty Ritchie says I hurt her hand when I press it — in the play, of course — because of her ring. I told her to remove it — the ring, that is, and she stepped back and said, "Naughty man! I shall tell my husband." I begged her to speak lower, and she said, "Oh, you wicked man!" I wish people wouldn't take ordinary jokes so seriously. It made me flush. I never meant anything, naturally. Women are odd.

Yours ever,
O . T H A K E

P.S. I implored Mrs Barlow not to call me Buddy, so now she says Bo, which is worse. Tell Saunders to tell cook I said only one policeman on Christmas Eve.

Woodgift House
Maidstone

A curious thing happened yesterday morning. I woke up at ten past nine — at least my clock said so. My wrist-watch said about twenty minutes past eight. I remembered winding one of them up the night before, but I thought it was the clock. But it couldn't have been, because that had stopped at exactly nine-ten. Whereas the watch, which said twenty past eight, was still ticking madly. I waited a bit, and then got up, only to find, on arriving downstairs, that the hall clock said a quarter to eight, so the watch and clock were both wrong, at least the watch was. The clock had merely stopped, as I say. The real time when I woke must have been about a quarter past seven, allowing for shaving and a bath, or, say twenty past. It all comes of letting Saunders go off to Epsom for the week-end with this fire-brigade chum of his. He should have come down here yesterday.

The rehearsals are all right. I begged Mrs Barlow not to call me Buddy or Bo, and now she calls me kid, which is worse. She got this American craze from a cousin or someone who's been in New York. She is trying to persuade them – the Watsons and Pierce, to include in the play a song called, as far as I remember, "When you see my Milwaukee Sweetie". Of course, we all objected, except Rose, who wants to be allowed to play her ukulele. All this would ruin the play. Mrs Watson and I are agreed that what is wanted is a straight drama. Tom called Rose a coon, and she cried, but I think they are going to let her play the barrel-organ in the big scene – off-stage, of course. A man called Harcourt has just turned up. Nobody seems to know him. He's in Tom's business, and makes paper kites for little Freddie. I must go now and rehearse.

Yours truly,
O. THAKE

P.S. Tell Saunders to tell cook policemen includes firemen on Christmas Eve, as far as I am concerned. This eyebrow stuff runs dreadfully.

Later.

After rehearsal today, I saw that man Harcourt in a corner with Mrs Barlow. Apparently she had got something in her eye, and he was trying to get it out. Perhaps this eyebrow stuff is giving her trouble, too. I told Tom Watson about it, but all he said was, *"Honi soit qui mal y pense."* I hope he didn't think I meant to say anything disparaging about the eyebrow stuff, which he recommended, though I must say it does run. He is rather touchy in some ways.

Woodgift House
Maidstone

What a season of the year, eh? I have been in town, buying trains for my nephews and dolls for my nieces. The shops seem to be full, don't they? However, we shall be having our dress-rehearsal of the play soon, and I'm getting quite into my part, but I wish there were more men in it. I seem to be surrounded by women all the time – I don't mean anything derogatory. I suppose that's the idea of the play, and of my name, Lothario. Didn't Sir Walter Scott (the Scott's Waverley novels man) write a poem about gay Lothario coming out of the west, or something? Or was it Byron? I hate putting the black stuff on my eyes. As I said, it runs and one looks odd. Mrs Barlow keeps introducing American phrases, and young Pierce, our author, gets very annoyed.

In all this gaiety I seem to be forgetting the more serious affairs of life. I shall have to make up for lost time in the New Year. I have hardly any time for reading. Isn't it desperate? But it's only once a year. Mrs Barlow doesn't use that eyebrow stuff, so it must have been a fly Harcourt was taking out the other night. She can't know him very well, because I heard her say to him last night, "Say stranger, what's eating you?" I was really most surprised.

I must go now and get a book for Rollo.

Yours truly,
O. THAKE

P.S. Tell Saunders he really must use his own discretion about where to put the mistletoe. Tom Watson says that the expression Mrs Barlow used to Harcourt is the American way of asking if anything is wrong. Really, a strange people.

Woodgift House
Maidstone

This is a short, hurried note. I'm all at sixes and sevens like the baker's dozen! Presents, the dress rehearsal, parties – Oh, dear! The dress rehearsal went off well. It is just the same as the actual performance will be, but, of course, without the audience. Otherwise, everything will be, or rather was, the same. Tom asked me if I was sure of my cues. I said, 'What! Queues in this show? Are there not enough seats?" But he capped my joke by saying, "No, billiard cues." Mrs Watson was annoyed and said we were delaying the action. Someone threw a holly berry at her – I think it was Aimée. So you see everybody is gay and festive. There's mistletoe up already – even in the wings of our little stage. It's rather difficult to keep clear of it. Women are so obtuse in some matters. They persist in standing under it. What an absent-minded sex. Why, Aimée even said to me, "Look, Mr Thake, at this mistletoe." I hardly knew what to reply. I think I said, "Yes, indeed," or something like that. Then they all laughed, and I pretended, in dumb show to be timing a golf shot.

Yours ever,
O . THAKE

P.S. Tell Saunders to tell cook policemen include not only firemen, but all other men, on Christmas Eve. Has he fed little Lion?

Woodgift House
Maidstone

Christmas comes nearer and nearer every day. One gets quite thrilled. Meanwhile we have got the play over. It was quite a success, and a curious experience for me. To begin with, there is a great difference between acting without an audience and with one – especially when all the people in it are so indistinct. You know they are there, but can hardly see them, and applause goes to one's head like old brandy. My line, "They call me dare-devil, and dare-devil I am, Lady Wrendeville," nearly brought down the Watsons' house. I hesitated at first, wondering if I ought to give an encore – that is, say the lines again. But Tom shouted from the wings, "This isn't a concert, you ass." I told him afterwards, pretty bluntly and plainly, that I wasn't silly enough to imagine it was a concert. "It's obviously a play," I added. To which young Pierce replied, "Not so much of the obviously, please." I meant no offence. Authors are so touchy. During the interval, Mrs Watson said to me, "Oswald, there's Katherine under the mistletoe." I pretended to have misheard, and replied, "Yes, very, for the time of year." What with one thing and another, where is one? I must go now and dress for dinner.

Yours ever,
O. THAKE

P.S. Tell Saunders to tell cook policemen, or no policeman, little Lion must be fed on Christmas Day.

❦ VII ❦

HONORIA BOLTONE

My DEAR BEACHCOMBER,

I'm afraid my wire did not explain fully enough what I meant when I asked you to tell Saunders – or rather to ask him whether it was King of Clubs I backed, and at what meeting? I meant to leave a margin of time to bet on the Grand National, if it was not that on which I betted originally. The wire meant that I had discovered it was the Lincoln I had betted on, and that therefore it was too late, or, rather, impossible for that bet itself to be on the Grand National. It was just a question of the two meetings, and my being doubtful which Saunders had put the money on for. Of course, seeing that it was the Lincoln, there was nothing to prevent me having another bet on the Grand National, provided I had been in time, unless he had put on both.

The man is queer. I gave him a month's warning in advance, that I wanted my Oxford tie for Saturday, and he promptly sends me – on Saturday night of all nights! – my brother's old regimental tie, green and brown. What on earth my brother's regiment has to do with it I cannot for the life of me decide. However, I have sent it back. It isn't as if my brother was still in the regiment. He's retired.

Do you know anything of a Mrs Boltone, a widow? She is staying here, and seems to me to be extraordinarily charming.

Yours ever,
O . THAKE

P.S. Tell Saunders to send some of those large sweets with alcohol in them.

I have to write seriously. You will wonder why I do not discuss foreign affairs, and say a word for or against the golf championship, the by-elections, Egypt, and the channel swimmers. Well, it is like this. I honestly think I'm in love. You will say it is the spring, as Lord Tennyson did. But no. It is Mrs Boltone herself, Honoria Boltone. The very name is like babbling brooks and budding branches. For long I have admired her, but now I know. Nothing is arranged, but I feel that we understand each other. We are neither of us children. When I asked her how old she as, she said, "As young as I look." And I believe her. She is the spirit of youth come to lay her hand on my fevered brow. She is serious, and not like the modern girls. We talk of many things and she plays the piano. When she asked me if I was rich, and I said, "What is money?" she agreed, and said she was glad I was not one of those horrible rich men.

We have been picking flowers. The things she says about flowers! Once she called a daisy a dream that had fallen from Paradise. Isn't that lovely? Oh!

What do I care now for Egypt, or the League? She is the only League I want. I do not even seem to want my meals, and at night when the moon is out, I read about Helen of Troy and swear to burn Hector's Palace for her. Honoria! Honoria! Honoria Thake! Will it ever be? I am unworthy of her I know. I have not even read her favourite poet, Swinburne, but she loves just what I love in Tennyson. In fact, all our tastes seem to be the same, and she is on a sort of local committee to support the Government. We were side by side on the platform the other day, and when she called me her Jupiter, I whispered back, "Juno!"

I am too full for words.

Yours ever,
O . THAKE

P.S. Tell Saunders to send me a copy of Swinburne, bound in calf – it is for a love token – (but don't tell him that).

De Courcy Manor
Lewes

This hand scarcely knows how to hold the pen. It – or rather I – have just come from the lawn, through the French windows, into the sunny room, where Honoria is playing the "Indian Love Lyrics". What a touch she has! I am not a sentimental man, but really, as she played I began to feel like the Indians in those songs. I said to her, "I could listen to you for ever."

"But I should grow tired," she answered.

"What matter?" I replied. "Besides, fairies do not grow tired."

"Am I like a fairy?" she said wistfully.

And as she rose she knocked a photograph off the piano, and in stooping, upset the piano stool. That brought Miss Felpham in, and by her looks she intimated that I had been guilty of a breach of good taste. I haughtily went out into the garden, where Honoria joined me amongst the tulips, and she the sweetest tulip of all. She told me about greenfly and how to mend lawn mowers, and as I listened I vowed to serve her for ever. In an ecstasy I knelt but she, with old-world grace, bade me rise, and herself wiped the hyacinth petals from my knees with the tiny square of cambric she carries so beautifully. In the evening, the Felphams left us alone as much as they could. Honoria recited to me. I almost proposed, but my tongue refused its office. Who am

I to aspire to a goddess? I am the veriest yokel in her presence. Her smile is my sun. And she is not coquettish. The only insect in my perfect amber is Miss Felpham, Tom's austere aunt. She again interrupted us as we were looking at "The Knitter's World" (March number) together. She said acidly, "The pleasure of an occupation in no sense connotes its propriety." But I walk on air.

Yours ever,
O. THAKE

De Courcy Manor
Lewes

Things move fast. I am almost whirled off my feet, but I do not complain. We have had a picnic on the downs, and Honoria and I have got to know each other even better. There were many incidents that put me in a seventh heaven, including one when we divided a hot-cross bun, wishbone fashion, and wished, I know what I wished, and I asked her to guess. She blushed and looked down, and I pressed my half into her hand jokingly, and our eyes met. In that instant – oh, I don't know. But anyhow, one day soon I am going to propose. I feel it in my bones, but whenever it seems to be the moment, my throat goes dry and I perspire.

Do you know a song called "Well-a-day"? To hear her sing it you'd think all the thrushes in the world were standing by the piano, pouring out their little hearts. I think I shall go mad – with joy, I mean, of course. You know. But it is worthwhile.

She has been asking me all about myself, and I told her about my school, and my second eleven cap for cricket, and my fives prize. Though fond of sport, she is not what you might call an athletic girl. She has a good service at tennis, but is too dainty for much work at the net; but to hear her say "Sorry partner," makes you want to commit suicide – momentarily, naturally.

I must stop. She is playing "Thora," and I must turn over for her. It makes me feel like a king.

Yours ever,
O . T H A K E

P.S. Tell Saunders to send my fives gloves to show her.

De Courcy Manor
Lewes

I have read somewhere that life is but a dream, or a sleep or something. Anyhow, it is for me. And I have made up my mind. Sooner or later I'm going to risk all, and put my fortune to the test. I mean I'm going to propose. The decision came to me yesterday, while Honoria was reading to me a passage from some paper about kitchen gardens. The passage described how one knows when a lettuce is ready to be plucked and brought to the table. It was not so much the subject, as her golden voice, and her evident love of domestic things. She said, "I would like a rabbit. I would call him Benson – my brother had one called that, and I would let him eat the lettuce, if he wanted to, poor thing. I would feed him myself." How I longed to say, "I would be your rabbit, your Benson," but, more practically, I promised to give her one.

She likes a lot of cupboards in a house, she says. I wonder if I could ever find one with enough. For she deserves a world of cupboards, Beachcomber. "The mountains look on Marathon, and Marathon upon the sea." Oh – I am full of bubbling poetry and melody. Bless her! "She is the miller's daughter, and oh, so fair and dear to me."

Well, well, I don't think her parents will object. They are very old, and would probably love to see their Honoria happy. Their Honoria? No, no. My Honoria. She has a tiny hand. I must buy her gloves. How far away my old political interests seem, but I must not wholly forget them. They will return, no doubt, as night follows the stars. You see, I am a sort of Tennyson these days. I never knew the trees were so beautiful. She has opened my eyes – "The sweet, sweet queen of my delight". Now I must take the *Fortnightly Review* to her on the lawn. Just an excuse for approaching her.

Yours ever,
O . THAKE

P.S. Tell Saunders to stop sending luggage labels. I never asked for any.

De Courcy Manor
Lewes

DEAR MR BEACHCOMBER,

When I was a girl, I was always told not to jump to conclusions. I sincerely hope my friendship, nay, my deep regard for Mr Thake is not leading people to talk. It is true that I forgot the Equine League meeting the other day, but it was a sunny day, and there are times when an attractive man can make one forget one's duty to the State. And, after all, I am not altogether sure that all this welfare work and committee business is not a little ridiculous. There are other things to do with one's time, and I feel distinctly rebellious, probably owing to the spring weather. Oswald says we should take a lesson from the lambs, who simply gambol, and care nothing about the cultivation of the civic virtues. Who knows but that he may be right?

I shall not speak on Teething at Hounslow next Thursday. Mrs Quagg has offered to deputise for me, as I have an engagement.

Yours sincerely,
HONORIA BOLTONE
(*née* Dipplethwack).

*De Courcy Manor
Lewes*

I really don't know how it all happened. I only know that she has consented to become Mrs Thake. There was a dance here last night, a fancy-dress affair. I went as Mark Antony, and she as a Dresden shepherdess. A fancy Dress-den shepherdess, as Tom Watson said wittily to old Burcraft. I kept on repeating to myself, "Faint heart never won fair lady," and "Nothing venture, nothing have," and so on. Well, during a waltz we sat out in the conservatory. She said, "Listen to this tune." I knew it well. It was "When I See That Look in Your Eyes".

"When I see that look in your eyes,
They mesmerize;
Don't you know I'm yearning?
Can't you see I'm burning,
All your love discernng . . ."

I said to her, "Honoria, I wish to speak."
"Speak what, Oswald?" she replied.
I turned to her.

"If," I said, "this conservatory were full of roses instead of all these ferns and chairs, I would heap them all upon you."

"It is the thought that counts," she answered.

Then, suddenly, she was in my arms. "Mine to treasure and to hold," I said.

"For ever," said she, lowering her lashes.

"Aye, for ever," said I, clutching her hand.

A miniature fountain on the left bubbled, as though in mirth and gladness.

I am going to my aunt's tomorrow for a day or two to tell her the glad news. Then I shall return and complete the arrangements. Now, will you give Saunders a very important message? He is to send direct to her a parcel which he will find in the top left-hand corner of my desk. It contains an album of all photographs of me, and my school reports. He cannot mistake the parcel. It is labelled "Private".

Well, Mrs Thake! There it is. My heart is too full for words.

Yours ever,
O. THAKE

P.S. Tell Saunders to register the parcel.

De Courcy Manor
Lewes

How doleful it is to leave the loved one, though it be for only a day or two. I never realized how terrible separation is, and to think that in a few hours I must leave her. Ah, how I yearn to protect her always in this hard world. I have received many congratulations already. Yesterday we wandered on the downs, care-free as two birds, and we planned for the future. She wants to be married at St. Mary's, and she shall have her wish. Also, she likes etchings, and mauve curtains for the dining-room. How sweet she is – like some shy young nymph, when I take her hand and say, "How lucky that numismatist (her first, and now luckily deceased husband) must have been!" Yesterday she said, "There are finer men, Oswald, than numismatists." And I said, "Dare I hope to be one?" I meant a finer man, of course; but she playfully saw the wrong meaning and chaffed me about Coué. Such playful trivialities are very lovely, I think. But then, everything in the world is lovely now.

Not a ripple disturbs the unruffled surface of the ocean of our love. Not a rock appears to bode shipwreck for our craft, which sails gaily towards Paradise with Cupid at the poop. Her eyes are like two planets that reflect their own glory. In them I read my destiny, and her arms are like arum lilies, and her lips like red chestnut blossom. I must go to her now, as our parting is near. I may be three days at my aunt's, but we shall have each other's photographs to look at. Ah, Beachcomber, love is life.

Yours ever,

O. THAKE

*The Forge
Old Withering*

The world is cold and empty as an iceberg. She has not written. I cannot think why she is silent. It is true that I have not been long away, but she vowed to write by every post, and to have the letters expressed. And now it is all dust and ashes and Red Sea fruit. What would I not give for a sight of that sweet calligraphy, and my own name written as only she can write it! Why is there no telephone at the Manor? I would wire to her reply paid, but how can one put into that buff envelope all the burning passion engendered by enforced exile from the Garden of Eden? A telegram would not lay bare to Honoria my palpitating soul, and she might think my love had waned.

How true it is that absence makes the heart grow fonder! Aye, a million years have rolled under bridges since I last stood in the sunshine of her presence. I have been reading "The Miller's Daughter," by Lord Tennyson, but can find little consolation in it. Every tap at the door brings my heart into my head; every ring at the bell sends me headlong from the room. But echo answers, "Nothing for you; only the man to see about the electric light in the study."

Now I know why lovers go mad, and commit suicide. Just a minute ago the bell rang again. I leaped up, trembling. They brought in a letter on a tray, but alas, it was only an ironmonger's circular. I could have flung it in the face of the maid, and cursed the very day ironmongers were created. My aunt is as sympathetic as she can be, and says, "The course of true love never goes as smoothly as one could wish." Yet in storm and stress 'mid peril and waiting, I will be true to her. Nothing shall deflect me, nor erode the purpose that arms me with steel. "Honoria," shall be my battle-cry. Besides, she must have reason for not writing, and I am cruel and uncharitable to blame her.

One can but wait and hope.

Yours ever,
O. THAKE

P.S. Impress upon Saunders that the parcel is marked "Private".

I have received from Mr Thake nothing but a telegram, the wording of which seems to indicate that he is extremely worried by the continual silence of Honoria Boltone. It runs thus: –

"Still no word Honoria shall go mad strain terrible can you or your paper throw any light on it all."

On receiving this I at once got into touch with Saunders. I asked him if he knew what was occurring, but he said that he did not. Incidentally, I asked him if he had sent off the package labelled "Private". He said he could only find one labelled "Very private," and had sent that off. I suppose that is the one my friend meant.

I wired later to Mrs Boltone saying: –

"Oswald prostrated write to him he begs for a word."

Her reply, which has rather mystified me, was: –

"Mr Thake shall hear from me in due course."

The whole situation was puzzling until I received the following letter from Mrs Boltone which speaks (quite loudly) for itself: –

De Courcy Manor
Lewes

DEAR MR BEACHCOMBER,

How foolish is a woman to put her trust in a mere man. Better for me would it have been had I stuck to committee work, and left the god of love to fend for himself. Here I am insulted. I had asked for Oswald's photographs and school reports. A package arrives, marked "Very private". With trembling fingers I open it, only to reveal the scorpion that I have been nursing in my bosom. I asked for bread, and he has sent me a stone by parcel post. What do I read? This: –

"Oswald dear, I count the hours till we meet again . . . I never knew what love was . . ."

And the hussy who dares thus flout my heart signs herself Letty.

I proceed. There are other letters, all proving that Oswald trifled with me. There is a Mrs Barlow, who refers to his "maddened embraces," an Agnes, who says the grip of his hand still burns her, a Greta who says that life without him is dross.

Yes, you will have guessed. I was the play-thing of an hour and he has cast me aside like an ill-fitting hat.

He has sent me all his old love letters from other women. Now, too late, I know the ignominy of man, and know that what I felt was not love, but infatuation. I am well rid of such a monster, whose false words still scald my derelict soul.

There are worse things: snapshots of him on the river with his horrible women; photographs of him smiling at them at the races, ski-ing with them at Wengen, walking with them at Cannes and Biarritz, motoring with them in the South of France. Need I say more? The golden dream is over. I am rudely awakened into an evil world – one more woman victim of these modern philanderers.

I can say no more. I will never speak to a man again. I will go back to the Softer Bits for Horses Society.

Yours broken-heartedly,
HONORIA BOLTONE
(*née* Dipplethwack).

On receipt of Mrs Boltone's letter I at once telephoned to Saunders. I asked him for an explanation and he said he thought a package marked "Very private" would be more likely to be the one than that marked "Private." So he had sent it along.

Meanwhile I have wired these facts to Mr Thake, and I shudder to think what it will mean to his sensitive and refined nature.

But what more can I do?

380a Jermyn Street
London, W—

My dear Beachcomber,

I am going away, to forget and forgive, if it be possible. Love's young dream, blighted and eaten by the greenfly of misunderstanding, lies a withered wreck at my feet. Fate has been against me, and just as the treasure was at my lips, it has been snatched and shattered by the rude hand of my valet Saunders. May he be forgiven for biting the hand that fed him. It is a warning not to expect too much. I, therefore, withdraw with as much dignity as I may, from all that the world held fair. Expect no more from me. In other lands, and under other skies, it may be, forgetfulness will come to me. Until that hour I shall sit in exile, by the waters of Babylon, having hung up my harp. I am the victim of circumstances. I go.

Yours ever,
O. THAKE

Amongst the crowd at Epsom yesterday stood a tall, thin figure, crowned by a tall hat rather rain-splashed. It was, I realized at once, Mr Thake. He turned a mournful eye on me as I approached, and I saw that he had not forgotten Honoria Beltone. As gently as I could I said, "What are you backing?"

In sepulchral tones he replied, "St. Mary's Kirk. We were to have been married at St. Mary's — not a kirk, of course, but an

English church. But I have no real interest in the race, beyond that name. Were there a horse called Beltone in the race, I would put my hat and coat on it for auld lang syne."

After a long pause he said, "Beachcomber, old friend of other days, one lives and learns. Experience comes to us all, and I think that even in suffering there is some profit. One rises stronger, like a sphinx from its ashes, and men may go over stepping-stones of their dead selves to something higher and better, like Maud in Lord Tennyson's poems."

"Will you dine with me at my club?" I asked.

"I do not dine," he replied. "You mean it well I know, but it is better so."

"Some other night?" I suggested.

"Who knows what other nights there will be? Who can probe fate, or foretell the future?" he retorted.

"Time heals all," I said, falling under the influence of his own style.

But he shook his head wearily, and moved away to talk to a bishop.

A few days after the Derby, I received the following letter from Mrs Boltone: —

The Lady Welfare Workers Club,
Victoria Street
London SW—

DEAR MR BEACHCOMBER,

I notice that my name was mentioned by Mr Thake at the Derby, and he said that he would put his hat and coat on a horse called Boltone, if he could find one. Allow me to state that no member of my family has ever given his or her name to a racehorse. As for Mr Thake's suggestion about putting his hat and coat on it, I leave it to vulgar minds to extract what meaning they can from a phrase so dreadfully *outré*. I can only add that if there is anywhere a horse bearing my name, I assuredly know nothing of the matter, and refuse to be dragged into it, to pander to the sentimental whim of a philanderer.

Yours truly,
HONORIA BOLTONE
(*née* Dipplethwack).

380a Jermyn Street
London, W—

I read, with some pain, the letter written to you by her whose name I still cannot say without undergoing pangs of grief. Cruelty follows cruelty. I offered her my hand. Does that sound like philandering? And now she suggests that I had some ulterior motive in searching for a horse bearing her name. She calls it vulgar. Is it vulgar to call a rose by a woman's name? Why should a horse become vulgar simply because this happens? She may say a horse is not a rose. Very true, but circumstances alter cases, as you will be the first to admit. Oh, dear, shall I never be understood? And is life naught but sack-cloth and ashes, bitter to the taste as vinegar? To be turned upon by the scorpion one nursed in one's bosom! To ask for a bit of bread, and to have a shower of stones flung at one! To knock at the door, only to have it slammed in one's face by the hand one is fed out of! Is this man's lot? If it is, it is a pretty bad one.

But I must not yield to self pity. Do you know of a good cook? This temporary woman is awful. She makes me think of Mrs Tinglebox, who, for all her faults, was a paragon. I'd get her back if I could. "I'll take her back, if she wants to come back, the cook who" – and so on – you know the song. Dear me, I am getting quite gay. "Smiles through tears," as the poet says, what? Ah, don't think, because I jest, that I have forgotten. Never, as long as the sun shines, shall I forget. The sea shall be dry land before I forget, and the dry land sea.

Adieu,
O. THAKE

Pansy Cottage
Reading

DEAR MR BEACHCOMBER,

The publicity that you gave to Mr Thake, with reference to me, is most annoying to me. I do not like to suggest that you are employed at a salary as his publicity representative, but there is obviously some agreement between you. I cannot open my mouth, without this gentleman – and gentleman I take him to be, in spite of his rather vulgar parade of the baser emotions – without, I say, this gentleman striking an attitude. There was never anything serious between us, at least not on my side. If I showed him any warmth of friendship, it was merely the mothering instinct that all true women have for helpless bachelors. May we not, at this juncture, consider the incident closed?

Yours truly,
HONORIA BOLTONE
(*née* Dipplethwack).

How much more than right William Shakespeare was when he said that ingratitude is worse than the teeth of serpents. Troubles never come singly. It never rains but it pours. I am being hit when I am down, and by her whom I thought as gentle as a dove. She calls love a base emotion, and accuses me of a vulgar parade of it. She calls me a helpless bachelor, as though I had two wooden legs and couldn't read or write. And then, worst of all, she says there was never anything serious on her side. What an actress – how grudgingly I write the word – what an actress she must have been? What about that dance at Mrs Felpham's, and the ten minutes of soft speech in the conservatory? How about her burning glance as we passed on the stairs? How about the entry in my diary which says, "Her hand is as cool as a lily on a pond by moonlight, and whiter than driven snow in the Arctic." Well? Well? And how about the hairpin she allowed me to keep after tennis at the Watsons'? Well?

Ah, how false is woman! And yet, I cannot blame her. I suppose I was presumptive. Love, love, what dost thou not do to us men? Eh? I must bury the past with a tear, and forgive her all the cruel things she says now of my sacred passion. I wonder how old Boltone won her. Ah, well. She need fear no more from me. I have loved and lost, like better men before me.

Yours ever,
O. THAKE

When I was a child I was taken to see a fortune-teller, who said, "You were born under a lucky star." She must have spoken with her tongue in her sleeve. Everybody seems to be against me. Am I to be pursued by all the relatives of the lady whose heart and hand I so recklessly sought, little deeming the consequences? Miss Dipplethwack, her sister, calls me a Lothario. Well, far be it from me to be a hypocrite. I admit I used to be rather a blade, you know, but what man isn't? Surely the ladies must take their share of blame for any success I may have had. Their bright eyes, what?

However, I get no peace here. The lift boys whisper when I come down to breakfast, and an actress has asked me for my autograph. A friend of mine, a curate, keeps bringing me the *Daily Express*, and saying, "Is that you, my dear Thake?" What can I do! A fellow called Swanscombe, with whom I played croquet once or twice, now cuts me, and his daughter edged away from me when I met her in Mrs Watson's drawing-room. The brother was there also, and made pointed speeches about evil-living adventurers. Really! What!

So once more against my will, I find myself the cynosure of all eyes.

By the way, my niece wants to go in for etching. Do you know the best thing to do about it?

Yours ever,
O. THAKE

Larch View
Surbiton

DEAR MR BEACHCOMBER,

I am not as young as I was, but, being Mrs Boltone's aunt, I do think that the members of a family ought to stand together. The allegations of this Mr Thake are so ridiculous as to make one doubt his sanity. The immodest proceedings he describes, such as hand-holding, seem to me to belong more to the privacy of the married state, than to the wooing of an honest man. From inquiries I learn that this man sent my niece a most immoral song, called, I think, "India's Love Lyric". One blushes for very shame.

Yours truly,
HELVETIA MIMMS

210 The Drive
Hindhead

DEAR MR BEACHCOMBER,

It was through my godson, Mr W. H. Rowden, of Beulah Hill, that I learned of the scandalous conduct of Mr Thake. The late Mr Boltone has only been cold in his grave for four years, but, as a spiritualist, I believe he will deliver a message that will make the evil-doer tremble. I am, I may add, a first cousin of Mrs Boltone, the wronged lady.

Yours truly,
HESTER SUFFIELD-CLAY

SIR,

Were I ten years younger, I would take my sword from the wall, and confront this debauchee with cold steel. That he should dare to calumniate my half-sister's good name!

Yours indignantly,
ALEXANDER WROTTE
(Lieut. Col.)

There are fourteen other letters, all from members of the family, and all written in the same strain.

380a Jermyn Street
London, W—

MY DEAR BEACHCOMBER,

Very well. Since I am to be persecuted by Mrs Mimms, the Colonel, and all the rest of them, let them all come, as the saying goes. Anybody would think that in holding her hand I intended an insult. But my mind is made up. I have written to Saunders, who is at the seaside, enclosing the pages of my diary, giving proof that the events actually occurred. The relations of her whose name I will not pollute by breathing it, seem to hint that I am telling lies when I describe her ardent glances, and her response to my handclasp in the conservatory. They shall be convicted out of my own mouth. Saunders has instructions to get carbon copies typed of these pages, and to send them, with a covering letter merely saying, "Perhaps this may convince you."

It is true I sent her the Indian Love Songs, or whatever they are called, but it was on the advice of my solicitor, whom I have known intimately for years. So the law at any rate, is allied with me in this matter. Where a solicitor sees no harm, it is not for others to cavil and carp. Evil to him or her who thinks evil.

Yours truly,
O. THAKE

*Larch View
Surbiton*

DEAR MR BEACHCOMBER,

With some surprise I received yesterday a letter from this Mr Thake. "Perhaps," said he, "this will convince you," and turning to the enclosed paper, I found that it was one of those seed catalogues from Haarlem, which would appear to be in Holland. Is this Mr Thake's idea of a joke, or is it a studied insult to the aunt of the woman he has wronged? In any case it is what one would expect from a notorious libertine. I notice that a certain species of rose was underlined in blue pencil. No doubt we have here one of those double meanings so dear to the frequenters of night clubs. Nor is this all. In the margin, opposite to some notes on lettuce, are scrawled in an ill-bred hand, the vulgar words, "Catch 'em young". A reference I suppose, to the shameless amours of this wicked man.

I shall not acknowledge his letter, believing, as I do, silence to be the only dignified retort for one who holds the honour of her family too dear to enter into brawling with a rake of this kind.

Yours truly,
HELVETIA MIMMS

380a Jermyn Street
London, W—

MY DEAR BEACHCOMBER,

Really, everything seems to get into more and more of a muddle. Anybody who knows me must realize that the seed catalogue was Saunders' mistake. Why should I send a seed catalogue? I know nothing about it, except that I have had a letter from an estate agent in Cumberland, a Mr Wright, enclosing the pages from my diary, and asking me what it all means. What can I tell him? It is all very absurd.

It is too unfair to refer to me as a dance-club frequenter. I have been once or twice with parties to the Great Western Hotel, but the dancing was over quite early. Besides, I expect "Catch 'em young" was written by the seedsman or his assistant, and probably referred to garden pests. Some people have evil minds.

That foolish Colonel Wrotte has sent me a solicitor's letter. I really don't know what it is all about; and a Mrs Spruce has sent me a parish magazine with my photograph in it, as No. VII. of the "Noted Adventurers," in the "Talks to Our Girls" column. All this is very flattering, doubtless, but it is going rather far. On top of it all, my niece has grown sick of the etching idea, and has gone and put me down on a Lighthouse Committee, somewhere on the East Coast, and an anonymous post-card, plain for all to read before delivery, has arrived, saying, "You are like the things they put in aquariums." Vulgar, and not funny.

Yours ever,
O. THAKE

2 North Delhi Mansions
North Kensington

SIR,

A sentence in General Fagsbury's memoirs seems to me to be most appropriate. He says, writing of the Puwari Campaign of '48, at which my father was present with old Scander: "The evil monster whom, for want of a better name, we call Moral Depravity." By the way, there was a fellow at Simla when I was a subaltern, and he carried on with a widow. Need I say that he was cut by the Mess and had to resign from all his clubs?

Yours truly,
ALEXANDER WROTTE
(Lieut. Col.)

Little Byre
Long Wiggling
Devon

DEAR MR BEACHCOMBER,

Pardon the liberty I take, but I live off the beaten track in Devonshire, and have only just heard of the plot against Mrs

Boltone, through my nephew, Hector. I need not say, that as Mrs Boltone's cousin, I am very much upset by the activities of this lawless philanderer, Mr Thake. A Mrs Parblow, who does such useful work in our village Institute tells me that he is a frequenter of night haunts. Can nothing be done to protect defenceless women from such dangers as are threatened by men like Mr Thake?

Yours truly,
DIMITY FLOOD (MISS)

*380a Jermyn Street
London, W—*

DEAR BEACHCOMBER,

Give a sheep a bad name and hang him for a lamb. The proof of the pudding is in the eating. Since everybody is so ready to heap calumny upon my head, I will jolly well justify my reputation. They shall all see what it would be like if I was really what they think I am, instead of being me as I am. Oh, I'm no child. I know more than some may think. Tonight, believe me or not, as you think fit – it is immaterial to me – tonight, I repeat, I am going to a cocktail party at a friend of Tom Watson's. I hear there will be chorus girls present after about eleven-thirty – *straight from their stage doors!* It is then intended to go on to a party at the Mixed Vermouth and then possibly to the house of a Mrs Sillingdale-Harvest, *who is separated from her husband!* I don't suppose we will break up much before *one a.m.* I am booked for a concert with Mrs Harvest next week.

I have ordered some of the new check ties, and one day next week, I am to drive about the West End in the car of a young girl called Edna. Oh, I have done with surnames – we are all hail-fellow-well-met in this set. Where did I meet Edna? Aha-a-a-a! That would be telling! No, but seriously, I was introduced to her at Rule's last night, by a man who has written a revue for the provinces. What was I doing at Rule's? Aha-a-a-a! I was there with a mica manufacturer and a girl, who they say, wore a bathing-dress at the Walmsley's amateur theatricals last year.

So there! You see I am as black as I am painted, eh? But do not think I forget her. In all the gaiety I see her face, and my heart grows heavy, in spite of the music, and the beat of gay feet. But I'll see it through.

Yours ever,
O . THAKE

P.S. Tell Saunders to send me a French novel called, I think, "Brillar-Saverin".

380a Jermyn Street
London, W—

What an evening! And it helped me to forget for an hour or two. The best fun was at Mrs Harvest's, whither we repaired about ten-thirty p.m. Sandra Mulrose, the half-Italian palmist, was there, and we pledged each other in foaming glasses. She took my arm – purely in friendship, of course, – and I winked at Mrs Harvest as much as to say, "Do not be jealous, I shall return to you." Then there was a man called Betchworth, who sang a sailor song and pretended to haul on ropes. Afterwards he did Indian clubs with two empty bottles of wine, and Phoebe Rushworth screamed, and swore one of the men had pinched her. I said I had, although, of course, I hadn't, and there was quite a hubbub about it, some laughing and others disapproving. Then somebody sang a rather questionable song called "I Passed by your Window".

We then went on to the Mixed Vermouth, which I was told was very Bohemian. A man in uniform was very rude to us because I toasted the whole room, and somebody else in evening dress told me to laugh less loudly. Also when I was dancing with Mrs Harvest, I hopped about a bit, just for fun, and I was again spoken to, this time by a man who asked me very pointedly whether I was a member. They took my drink away at eleven, because I refused to have a six-course supper, not being very hungry. Finally, Tom Watson made a hunting noise, and we were all asked to leave. "If a man can't cry 'Tally-ho' in a night club," I said loudly, "I don't know what England is coming to." They said they wanted none of my back-chat. I said, "It is not back-chat. It is common sense."

What a night! Really!

Yours ever,
O . THAKE

380a Jermyn Street
London, W—

You will not hear from me for some time. Now that I have lived life to its full, drained its cup to the dregs, tasted of its bitter fruit, and seen it in all its ugliness, I have decided to go away into retirement, and devote myself to the writing of a novel based on my experiences. Dear me!

Yesterday I went to the Theatrical Garden Party. That is one of the things that decided me. I walked about, quite unobtrusively, but everybody seemed to recognise me. Sir Gerald du

Maurier wanted me to take part in some play or other. Mr Leslie Henson asked if I could do any tricks, and a perfectly beautiful lady whose name I didn't catch tried to get me to sell perfume. It was all most embarrassing.

Here and there small knots of people cheered me, and I raised my hat as though I expected such manifestations. And while I was eating strawberries a hand was laid on my arm, and I was asked to sign my autograph. Really! "Am I Hobbs?" I said laughingly. "No," came the answer. So I wrote my name with as good a grace as possible.

When one has loved and lost one must grit the teeth. I am going away, as I said, to unburden my heart on paper – Tom Watson knows a publisher called Froome and Co. – and I hope you will not take it amiss, if, from time to time, I send you a passage or two for your criticism. I prefer to leave no address (except that I will give it to you in private), since I am far too well known for my peace of mind.

Good-bye and all good go with you.

Yours ever,
O. THAKE

P.S. Tell Saunders to send my snakeskin belt, and some of the long nibs from the study.

❧ VIII ❧

The Exile of Lido –
A Venetian Interlude

MY DEAR BEACHCOMBER,

Here I am, but I prefer to remain incognito – as they would say here – for purposes of writing. I am at the Excelsior Palace Hotel, where I bathe and lie in the sun. At a restaurant called the Terrazza I ran across Tom Watson, but as he began to tread on delicate ground, I said I had to be in Chioggia within an hour, and left him. After bathing I go over to Venice, whose beauty only reminds me, and opens old wounds, so do not think my address betokens frivolity. Was not Byron misunderstood? Did he not frequent gay gatherings, and yet stand apart with his dreams? I am not Byron, I know, but I too have known. Often as I feed the pigeons in the piazza, I say to myself, "My dear sir, my *dear* sir" – but really, I don't know. A man called Wrench, who collects stamps, says Time heals all. I doubt it. "Beauty hurts," I retorted, to which he rejoined, "Catch 'em young, treat 'em rough, and tell 'em nothing." Vulgar, vulgar, vulgar. Eugh! However:

There are so many churches in Venice (should I say on Venice, since it is a sort of island) that one begins to think the place must have been all monks and nuns once. One can hardly keep pace in the book with what the guides are saying. But when the moon is in the heavens and the night is settling down, one sees a gondola glide along the surface of the deep, one tastes the sour grapes of life. Even Venice may have naught to offer the hungry soul. But, faugh! (not in the golfer's sense!) Why repine? Let us smile bravely through the mist. I'm for a *strega*, and then I'll snap my fingers. A fig for it all, say I. Yet, I don't know.

Yours ever,
O. THAKE

Venice is a curious place. Yesterday, as I was having an *aperitif* at Florian's, and gazing at the clock over what they call the Merceria, who should come up to me but Aimée Boyle. She is apparently here with Webster's cousins, not the Ramsgate ones. They – the Ramsgate ones I mean – are in France. But I only tell you all this, because the point is that she is staying in my hotel on the Lido without my knowing it. She asked me why she had not seen me dancing there in the evenings, and I said I had no heart for dancing. She told me Ellaline, her sister, had married "Bops" Herringay, and I said I didn't much care. She reproached me with being cold and distant, and reminded me that I once gave her a fountain pen. I said, 'I don't see what that's got to do with it." Women are so illogical, not that I blame them. They wouldn't be women if they weren't.

I was in a gondola yesterday, but lost my stick.

There is a tiresome man here who will call me "Governor". It is most annoying. And he winks at me. He is with a party of queer people, and he offered me some of the medicine out of one of their bottles at lunch the other day. He said I looked blue, and I retorted that my colour was my own affair, which made one of his party titter. The girls in his party are worse. They shout, "Charleston Joe," whenever I go out. I shall complain to the proprietor if it goes on.

Betty Ritchie is here, and eats in a bathing dress. And even she put a pack of cards in my hat the other day. Everybody is so frivolous and silly here.

Yours ever,
O. THAKE

I can no longer remain anonymous here, for this reason, that I had forgotten my name was in the hotel register, and on my trunks, and has appeared in a local paper. Now, another matter. I am inclined to go to the Consul here, to lodge a complaint. It's about these awful people who keep trying to hobnob with me. I have discovered their name is Whiddy, and the girl they call "Chick," who shouts "Charleston Joe!" at me, is a sort of actress. She acted in a kind of show here a short while ago, with a thing called a spot-light, and she picked me out and sang a terrible song at me, something about "Naughty Eyes on a Summer Night". I have been trying to compose a letter to the Consul, but it is so difficult to put things in a dignified way.

If I had not changed my hotel, I should never have had this trouble, but I had to do so because Aimée Boyle became rather impossible. And the other people spent so much time at the Excelsior Palace Hotel that I thought they were staying there, but, to my horror, I found after I had established myself here that this is their headquarters. I can hardly change again. Perhaps a personal interview with the Consul would be better, explaining how all this winking and the rest of it inconveniences me. The dreadful father poked me in the ribs with his umbrella this afternoon, and said, "Having a good time, Guv'nor? I'm glad you've moved over here near us." I replied with a complete silence.

The youngest boy is a perfect devil. He will keep sticking bits of stamp-paper on my coat when my back is turned, and the family seems to think it funny. The page-boys keep reminding me that the stuff is on my back, and an American girl asked me last night if I was going to post myself back

home. I bowed and said, "The laugh is on me, dear lady."
What else could I have said? Later I saw her outside the Luna,
and she shouted something at me, to which I answered, "To
amuse you is an honour."

Every moment I dread to hear the shout of "Charleston Joe!"
It destroys my nerves. I shall have to leave if it goes on.

Yours ever,
O . THAKE

*Grand Hotel
Lido*

It is no good. I shall have to go. Can I never find peace
anywhere? This frightful family will not let me alone. Today
the daughter put a label on my back saying, "Glass, with care." I
ask you! What is a man to do? That silly Mrs Floss said to me, "I
see you are made of glass." I said, "I really don't know what on
earth you are talking about." She said, "Look at your back." I
said, "How can I? I am not a walking mirror." She said, "Perhaps
you are. Mirrors are made of glass." I said angrily, "That may
well be." And then Lord F ___ took the label off my coat, and
showed it to me. I tore it up, amid absurd laughter. It is all very
well, but one can't write to a British Consul about that kind of
thing. It's too much.

Really! I am going away somewhere else. The thing is
impossible. How right my Aunt Minnie was when she used
to say that unless one is understood, life becomes impossible.
How right, indeed!

I went to Murano yesterday to see the glass-blowing, and
that dreadful father of the girl said, "I bet you can't blow a
conservatory, Mr Thake." I declined, and he jeered, saying, "If

you blow a greenhouse, I'll blow glass tomatoes," – and in front of the natives, too. I am going away out of all this blowing of tomatoes and other nonsense. I must have peace. Do you see?

Yours ever,
O.THAKE

✦ IX ✦

THE WAVELINGS

MY DEAR BEACHCOMBER,

I must trust to your recognizing my writing, as I prefer not to have my name bandied about. I am writing to tell you of a curious coincidence that has occurred to me here at the hotel. I have been introduced to a Miss Waveling, who writes pamphlets for an animal society, I forget which. Her sister, whom they call Barbara, whose cousin got a D.S.O. on the Somme, in, I believe, 1916 – but that is unimportant – well, this girl apparently met you some time ago at the house of some people called Faddle. He, the Mr Faddle, was, I think, a musician, and lived in Somerset or Norfolk, I am not certain which. Anyhow, the point is that Miss Waveling's sister, Miss Barbara Waveling, has written an article about apples (or perhaps it's oranges) which she thought might be published in some paper. Now at present, she has lent the article to a Mrs Bruce to read, because this Mrs Bruce has a friend who does the poultry gossip for a local paper in Cumberland. So far, so good.

The point is, if this Miss Barbara Waveling gets her article back from Mrs Bruce with the opinion that the friend could not use it – in any case, he is away in Italy – do you think, if she sent it to you, you could do anything about it? It is about four thousand, four hundred words long, and she wants to put on the top of it, "By the author of 'Love's Morn'," which was a story she wrote for a cycling paper last November, but which was never accepted. She calls the article "Apples" (or "Oranges" – I forget which), but, of course it could be altered, as long as she saw a proof, and it must be copyright in all countries. If it is not troubling you too much, could you drop a note saying yes or no to E. N. Sprott, her cousin, at The Briars, Hobble Cross, Sussex, and he will let her know.

Yours ever,
A. FRIEND

P.S. Tell Saunders not to send any more biscuits. I can buy anything I want here. Anyone would think I was starving.

Hotel des Fous du Monde
Deauville

DEAR MR BEACHCOMBER,

As soon as I heard that Mr Thake had approached you with a view to getting an editor to publish my sister's article, I determined to write and thank you. We met, you may remember, at the Faddles' last October. Now, what I want to tell you is this: my sister is naturally very modest, and you must not take her at her own value. She is an excellent writer, and has received warm praise from Miss Bundle, who wrote "Desert Passions". Miss Bundle read a sketch of my sister's about ways of nailing down carpets, and offered to show it to the editor of "Wickerwork". But my sister was too shy, and could only just be persuaded to let the vicar have it for his parish magazine. If your editor likes "Oranges," make her send him "The Soot Menace," which is a scathing indictment of coal, from the point of view of one who hates industrialism.

We all like your friend Mr Thake. Alas! he seems a lonely and unhappy man. He carries about with him a copy of Lord Tennyson's "Maud," and sometimes reads to us Mr Meredith's "Love in the Valley". He also seems considerably worried by packages and letters he receives from England. I hope nobody is menacing him. He certainly gets odd things.

Poor man. He asks me to say to you that he is writing shortly, and will you tell Saunders there is some mistake about the bill for butterfly nets, as Mr Thake never bought any.

Yours gratefully,
HESTER WAVELING

Appledene
Near Southborough
Kent

DEAR MR BEACHCOMBER,

Pardon this liberty I take in writing to you, but I have heard of Mr Thake's great kindness to my two sisters, and I hear he is sending you an article of Barbara's, which you are going to get published. Now I wonder if you could help me. I am sending one or two of my drawings to Mr Thake, asking him his advice about getting them accepted. One is of Scarborough, and another of Bexhill, so you see they are quite topical. I have also sent to Mr Thake a piece of verse called "Thistles," which is by my best friend Vera Randall. We were at school together, and she writes divinely. I'm sure any editor would be glad to publish it in his paper. Of course, Barbara is the really clever one in our family, and we are dreadfully proud of her. She wrote something about soot and its menace, which dad said would get her a scholarship if she were a boy. I've no training, so you must forgive the mistakes in my work.

Vera says that if you and Mr Thake like "Thistles," she has a small series of flower-poems, which she could send later, and she has a friend whose brother is awfully clever at inventing puzzles – the sort they print in newspapers, you know. She is sending one or two of them to Mr Thake with the pictures and the poem. He must be an awfully kind man to take all this trouble. Barbara says he's very distinguished and very gloomy, like Byron. He sounds fearfully thrilling and romantic. I should love to meet him, and perhaps I shall, if he comes to us in England, when the holiday's over. Barbara says he collects queer things, like butterfly-nets.

Thank you so much.

Yours sincerely,
FELICIA WAVELING

Hotel des Fous du Monde
Deauville

DEAR BEACHCOMBER,

Shakespeare says somewhere that there is a destiny that shapes our ends, no matter how roughly we hew them. How true it is in my case! Wherever I go, and whatever I do, I seem to meet trouble. I scarcely know which way to turn at present. My room here is like Bedlam. I have got Miss Barbara Waveling's confounded article, which isn't even typed. Then there are her sister's idiotic drawings, Miss Vera Randall's poems, which I don't understand, some young man's puzzle problems, two short stories from some other man, a one-act play from a woman called Grabbham, a ballet from her brother, and an essay on the Patriotism of Byron, by an undergraduate. And all this nonsense started because, in an unguarded moment, I promised Miss Hester Waveling I would do my best for her sister's writing. The thing is impossible. She seems to have told everybody that I am a sort of god in the literary and artistic world. Only this morning a letter arrived from a girl I've never heard of asking my advice about contralto songs. Really!

I am forwarding all this stuff to you. For pity's sake, use as much of it as you can, or they will blame me. I simply dread the post now. For all I know, there may be more members of the Waveling family lurking about. Whenever I meet the eldest sister, she gives me no peace, but at once talks literature. I flatter myself that I am a cultured man, but I cannot bear being asked, immediately after breakfast, what I think of Thackeray. There is a time for everything, and this is overdoing it.

Yours ever,
O . THAKE

P.S. Tell Saunders he must be mad to send me diving-boots. They are entirely useless to me. I don't see the point.

By the same post as Mr Thake's letter, I received a mass of material, nearly all of which is utterly amateurish. But I suppose I must use some of it, to save my old friend's face. Therefore I choose the following, without apology:–

THISTLES
BY VERA RANDALL

They grow upon the hillside,
   And nod before the breeze;
O Thistle, thistle, thistle,
   Do not prick my knees.

And when the night is falling
   And all the world is still,
I see the thistles standing
   Alone upon the hill.

Beloved, it is better,
  In meadow or in mart,
To have thistles on the hillside
Than thistles in the heart.

*Windyridge
St. Ospic's Bay
Norfolk*

DEAR MR BEACHCOMBER,

Although I appreciate deeply the kindness of yourself and Mr Thake, and my friend Felicia Waveling, in taking an interest in my work, you can imagine with what a shock I opened my *Daily Express* only to find that "Thistles" contained a serious error. Line three of Verse one reads, "O Thistle, thistle, thistle". It should, of course, read, "O Thistle, gentle thistle". The adjective accentuates the appeal to the herb not to prick the knees of the victim, and avoids the repetition of one word three times. I should like your editor to publish a letter of apology, together with the correct version of the poem. My cousin (you have probably heard of him), Randolph Gower, is a solicitor, and he says it is most important to stick up for one's rights, especially on beginning a career. He says one might almost get damages for such a misrepresentation.

I trust you will put it right. I enclose a little sketch by my friend Ursula Stock. Do use it if you can.

Yours always,
VERA RANDALL

I wonder what on earth the Waveling sisters imagine a newspaper of-
fice to be like. I have just received another letter from Miss Hester
Waveling, enclosing two preposterous drawings by a small nephew,
aged four. She describes them as "clever and original drawings, with
a topical interest," and tells me that the boy's mother is a vegetarian.
The sketches are called "King Gorje Shoting," and "Southend
Pear". The King's felt hat is surmounted by a crown, and "South-
end Pear" begins on one sheet of paper, and continues on the back
of the same sheet, after the notice P.T.O.

I have space to quote only the P.S. of Miss Waveling's letter: –

. . . So I hope you will publish the drawings. The one of the pier
at Southend is a difficulty, but I suppose you have machinery in
your office whereby you can overcome the unusual idea of
continuing a drawing on the back of a sheet of paper. I think it
would be nice to leave the spelling unaltered. It would please the
little lad, and also his parents, one of whom is my brother. The
boy's name is Yglesias Hibb, if you care to use it. My brother
changed his name to Hibb a year ago – none of us ever knew
why . . . Barbara is sending you an article on darning-needles.

Hotel des Fous du Monde
Deauville

DEAR BEACHCOMBER,

I hope you will realize that I only write this under pressure, in
order to secure a little peace from these dreadful Wavelings. It is
this. Miss Hester – I mean Barbara Waveling – wants you, if
possible, to publish the article about darning-needles which I
enclose, instead of her one about the oranges. She also wants you
to put her sister Hester's name on it, as well as her own, as her

sister helped her with it, and wrote some of the phrases towards the middle – for instance, the one about a darning-needle being a woman's *vade mecum*. I have been trying to keep out of their way, but cannot. I shall have to leave here, I fear. In fact, I'm not sorry that the time is near at hand when one can return to London. The fifteen novels Mrs Wretch sent me are driving me mad. She must be a tiresome woman.

I forgot to mention that the poem enclosed is by Barbara Waveling – no, Felicia Waveling, and that it is to be included in the article, and that her name, too, is to appear at the top of it – so all three of them must be mentioned as authors – the three witches in Macbeth, eh?

It would be very pleasant here without all this worry. The blue sea laps against the shore, the sky is blue also, and occasional gulls wheel about in the soft air. The nights are serene and dark, save when the moon gilds the scene. I venture to send you a poem I wrote about it all – but don't think I have caught the fever from these women, please! But I saw one by Vera Randall, and I think this is just as good.

Yours ever,
O . THAKE

P.S. Tell Saunders I do not want the address of any more glass-blowers. I never asked for any such thing.

NOCTURNE
BY O. THAKE

When I gaze up at the fair moon,
I fall into a sort of swoon;
It seems to be the beauteous face
Of her who haunts my nights and days.
And every star that shines above

Is like the eye of my true love.
And every pool that shines below
Is like her voice so soft and low.
And everywhere I look at all
I seem to think I hear her call.
Ah no! It is an idle dream.
Things are not, they can only seem.

*Mr Thake, whose many troubles force me to make allowances for him, en-
closed in his last letter Miss Barbara Waveling's article entitled "Oranges" instead of the one about darning-needles. I, therefore, publish as
much of the former as possible. It was nearly five thousand words in
length, but I have tried to cut it down judiciously. I think it shows great
promise. Here it is. (The dots are mine, and mark my "cuts".)*

ORANGES
BY BARBARA WAVELING

. . . Little spheres that seem to hold cloistered in their depths all
the bright sunshine of Spain, all the stored colour of that *laissez-
faire* land of señors and señoritas, bulls, guitars and priests . . . As
one walks beneath the swaying orange trees of Seville, hearing
on all sides the lazy Spanish tongue, one cannot help being struck
by the thought that all these acres of fruit will one day be
marmalade in our gloomier northern homes . . .

. . . The child who spreads this delicious condiment on his or
her bread does not dream that he or she is about to absorb the
sunny south, land of passion and romance, land of hot tempers,
hasty words, and knives suddenly produced from stockings . . .
land of . . . land of . . . Thus are Spain and England for ever
linked in a common bond of friendship . . . and . . . and . . .
and . . . so that . . . for ever . . . heritage . . . friendship . . .
Then there are the great pipless oranges so dear to those who find
pips a deterrent to the enjoyment of this . . . fruit.

. . . A great man once called oranges the solace of jaded palates. And indeed . . . Oranges are a reminder that the fruits of earth were given to man for his delectation . . . I never look at one without seeing the white-walled towns of that land of . . . land of . . . and hearing the mule bells in that land of . . . land of . . .

I think I have kept the sense of the thing, without sacrificing too much of the really beautiful prose. I was forced to omit the long passage about using orange skins to clean oak panelling, and the still longer one about orangeade at Henley.

Hotel des Fous du Monde
Deauville

DEAR MR BEACHCOMBER,

I hoped I should be in time to rectify Mr Thake's mistake. I wanted the darning-needle article published first, but he sent you the orange one. That, in itself, is distressing, but judge of my horror on seeing how you had mutilated my work, and had not even put copyright below, nor, "By the author of 'The Soot Menace,' etc., etc., etc." above it. As to copyright, my sister Hester says that the Americans are rather unscrupulous in that way, and might print the article, or parts of it, in one of their papers without acknowledgement – a compliment, no doubt, but not what I should care to happen.

But the mutilation horrifies me. I did not know that newspaper men behaved so scandalously, and in future I shall confine myself to novels and short stories. No doubt it is the system's fault, and not yours.

Dear Mr Thake seems very *distrait*. Hester asked him where he was going to next, and he almost shouted "Samarkand!" He is worried still, I think, and is frequently receiving dummy Post Office Directories, with nothing inside. After reading his poem, I imagine he has had an unhappy love affair, the poor man. I think some lunatic is in touch with him, otherwise why does he keep all those queer things in his room? When Hester and I had tea with him in his suite we saw the quaintest collection – butterfly-nets, bicycle-clips, cardboard eggs, potato-mashers, harpoons, diving-boots, and even a coil of barbed wire. He is a queer man. Have all those things sentimental associations for him?

Yours sincerely,
BARBARA WAVELING

Hotel des Fous du Monde
Deauville

I notice that a novelist has been defending himself against the accusation of having put real people into his books. Now it seems to me that I come into this. Whatever I do, and wherever I go I am chattered about. I have just been reading the remarks of that intolerable Miss Waveling about me. Not content with telling the world that my room is full of barbed wire and cardboard eggs, she hints that these articles may have a sentimental association for me. How absurd! How could they have? And the other day, when I had dodged a journalist who was after me, up came the sister Hester, and told him my favourite colour is blue, that I smoke Egyptian cigarettes, and that my lucky day is Wednesday. Also an artist here named Stavehold-Gault has drawn me, and put the thing up for auction in the hotel lounge. Really!

Mrs Wretch herself has arrived here, and is for ever fussing about her novels. She comes and takes her coffee at my table, and is always asking me whether I think character is internally or externally self-revealing, and what my opinion is of ultra-expressionism as understood by Smallfish and his school. As if I knew or cared! It is all double Dutch to me. I am off soon, thank goodness. My luggage will be absurdly bulky. Saunders, for some reason best known to himself, has sent me five thousand leaflets about clover. It is all very mysterious.

Yours ever,
O.THAKE

❖ X ❖

MADAME LA COMTESSE

MY DEAR BEACHCOMBER,

My attention has been called to an article in the Press of England, attacking the game of bridge. I am surprised at anybody being so reactionary, so to speak, and I feel that I must protest, because I play a good deal out here, and, therefore, should be a hypocrite if I passed over this scurrilous slur in silence. After all, the honour of those who play it with me is at stake. So please regard this protest as official.

We are a merry party at the hotel, and after a hard day on the rink or on skis, we enjoy our game of bridge. I usually have for a partner a most likeable young lady, a French widow, whose husband was in a cavalry regiment, and was killed, she tells me, in Nicaragua, during the riots there, while leading his regiment. Her name is Comtesse Germaine Eulalie Nicolette Cécile de Mont-Saint-Brignolles-le-Vaurien, a very old family, and she is every inch a Comtesse.

Yesterday she played against me with a young Russian. She said she must occasionally desert me for another partner, to prevent the long tongue of scandal wagging. As though by fate, I lose heavily every time she is against me. Therefore I called her my *mascotte*, which is French for mascot.

We were on the Kulm rink yesterday, and she showed me how to waltz on skates. And every time I took her hand, she said, with delightful banter, "Now, now, Monsieur Thake, that is not necessary, you know." I explained that one had to hold one's partner's hand in a dance, and she said, "I know that, Sillee Bille, but one need not squeeze it." To which I replied with mock solemnity, "Madame la Comtesse misconstrues my intentions," and we both laughed.

I only mention such incidents to show how merry and happy we all are here. And then, like a lightning stroke out of a clear sky, comes that bridge bombshell! I thought of writing a defence of it today, but other pleasures claim me. The Comtesse and I and two others are to go down the Cresta Run to Celerina today.

Tonight there is a fancy-dress dance. I will tell you of it tomorrow.

Yours ever,
O. THAKE

P.S. Tell Saunders to send me a copy of Derrick's "Bridge Wisdom".

Hotel Albernheit
St. Moritz

I write to you with the lilt of the dance still in my ears. The ball was a great success. I went as a French porter, in a black mask, of course, and there were two people called Foote, who made a sensation as Homer and Florence Nightingale. The Comtesse made a divine shepherdess, with blue ribbon tied round her crook. Later in the evening – purely as a joke, I need hardly tell you – I attempted to tie this ribbon into a true lover's knot, but the thing got muddled. She laughed and said, "But, Monsieur, what is it you try there?" I replied, "A mere bagatelle, Comtesse, a nervous habit."

During the earlier part of the evening I could not get away from a woman called Hurtle. She was supposed to be a Begum, and kept on talking about her daughter, who is trying to be a female chartered accountant somewhere in Scotland. Finally I lost her. After I had brought her a glass of lemonade, I said hastily,

"I promised the next dance to my sister." She said, "I should like to meet her," which made me very uncomfortable, as, of course, I haven't one – at least not out here. Then something very romantic happened. The Comtesse, in passing near me, said:

"Be under the chandelier by the window that opens on the terrace at 11.50."

"I will," I murmured, and, gay at the prospect, attempted to Charleston with the Begum.

At 11.50 I went to the trysting-place, and there she was. Together we moved from the room, and, she in her cloak, and I in my overcoat, went out on the terrace.

"Let me carry your crook," I said, but she refused.

The whole world was bathed in moonshine, and there stood the untrodden snows, where but yesterday we had tobogganed – cold and eternal and far-reaching.

"We can unmask now," I said.

"Unmask?" said she, "I wonder. When the piece of black is removed, is there no other mask there? *Hein?*"

"Maybe not," I retorted, her mystic words and pulsing voice well-nigh upsetting me.

I stepped close to her, to remove her mask, but got the elastic twisted.

"Clumsy," she said.

"A sign of a warm heart," I replied.

The strains of "Red Hot Momma" were wafted to us, as we leaned over a balustrade, side by side.

"Amuse me," she said. "Be witty."

So I did that trick of mine of moving the ears.

She laughed.

"My hand is cold," she said.

"It is the night air," I replied.

"Let me put the hand in the pocket of your overcoat," she said.

"Beauty commands," I answered.

The band was playing "Sugar Daddy o'Mine," and I said, "It is time to dance. These walls have eyes."

So we went back. Was not the whole thing romantic?

Only one misfortune marred the night. I lost an amber cigarette holder, which must have fallen out of my overcoat pocket.

Yours ever,
O. THAKE

Hotel Albernheit
St. Moritz

Yesterday it snowed hard, and instead of going out, I decided to spend the day by the fire in the lounge with a novel called "Barchester Towers". I was pleasantly interrupted by a message from the Comtesse, asking if I would care to lunch in her suite. I accepted with alacrity, and after the meal, she offered to teach me a new card game. It was a curious game, which I could not quite follow, and she was sweet enough to offer to return the money she had won. Naturally I refused.

"Comtesse by name," I said to her, "and Comtesse by nature. You are too charming."

At that she half-closed her eyes, and said, "You find me charming?"

"Utterly," I retorted, and upon my soul, it was on the tip of my tongue to say words even more passionate. She must have read my thoughts, for she leaned towards me, and said, "What is utt-er-lay?"

"Something very big," I said, stretching out my arms to illustrate my meaning.

But she, dear innocent Comtesse that she is, saw in the gesture rather more than I meant her to see. Drawing back, with a little scream, she said, *"Mais non, Monsieur! Oh, mon Dieu!"*

I begged her pardon, and explained that what she took for violence was merely measurement.

Finally I read her "The Wreck of the Hesperus," and told her about my journey to Dublin in a storm, when Tom Watson lost his gloves overboard. She then went to the piano, and sang a song called, "Plaisir d'Amour," which means in French, of course, pleasure of love.

In the evening she told me her husband had left her a sort of mine somewhere in the Caucasus, and she offered me a number of shares. I could not find out what kind of mine it was, as women do not study these things, but from her description, it was iron ore, or something. I signed a paper and became the proud owner of quite a lot of shares at really rather a cheap figure. She says they are sure to go up, as the peasants there need ore. The only trouble is that bad luck continues to balance her great kindness to me. I have lost the silver cigarette-case the Worshipful Company of Glassblowers gave me, and also my links. It is most curious.

Yours ever,
O. THAKE

P.S. Tell Saunders to send out some links and a cigarette-case, and also pearl studs for the shirt-front, as I have lost mine – and also a button-hook. My silver one seems to be missing.

Hotel Albernheit
St. Moritz

Who was it, I wonder, who said, "Pleasure costs us dear"? How true it is! I am really rather worried by my heavy losses at cards, yet the pleasure of her company is so great that what can one do? She keeps teaching me new card games, and I nearly always bungle. But she wins with such a good grace that one cannot complain without appearing a churl. Nor are card losses my only trouble. I have lost the valuable fountain-pen given me by the Ancient Order of Emus.

I have been polishing up my skating and ski-ing, as the Comtesse has half-persuaded me to go in for the Celerina Cup and the Kulm Medal. I may just secure last place in the English ice-hockey team too – though I still get rather confused between figures of eight and shots at goal.

How gentle she is! How gentle! Yesterday I fell over on the rink. In a moment she was at my side with brandy. I was soon none the worse, save for the loss of the new cigarette-case Saunders sent out. She explained that it must have slipped through a hole in the ice. She offered me her arm as we went off the rink, and everyone applauded.

She told me today that, as she knew me better, she wanted to let me have some shares in another concern of her late husband's – a company formed to make park railings out of some cheaper form of iron. She said orders were pouring in to her solicitors, so I bought some shares. If all goes well, I ought to be able to get back all I have lost at cards and more.

We went to Pontresina yesterday, and there we played cards again. It is extraordinary, her love of the game. I lost, and in fun, accused her. I said, "Madame Germaine, you must have two aces of diamonds." She went quite pale, which shows how sincere she is, and it took me some time to explain that I was only joking.

"It is a funny joke," she said, frowning.

"All our English jokes are funny," said I, beaming at her.

So we shook hands, and she held on to my right one, and said, "How rare men are!"

"And women too," I retorted, touching her left hand.

All our companionship is full of these romantic moments.

On returning home, I discovered, to my intense anger, that I had lost a signet ring. She, with that self-sacrificing generosity of hers, insisted on going back to Pontresina there and then, in the cold, to hunt for it. But we never found it.

"Such is life," I said.

"*Mais oui*," she answered.

She is irresistible.

Yours ever,

O . T H A K E

P.S. Tell Saunders to send out my other brushes. My silver-backed pair has disappeared.

Hotel Albernheit
St. Moritz

The ice-hockey match took place yesterday. I was bitterly disappointed at not being chosen for the team, but luckily one of the team was down with 'flu. Encouraged by the Comtesse, I eagerly suggested to the captain that I should take the place of the casualty. He went off to consult with the other players. They were obviously pleased at the chance offered, for they laughed a good deal, and one of them said, "What do you play for?" I said I was purely an amateur, and played just for pleasure. He said, "I mean, what club?" I told him that, at the moment I was not playing for any club, but that I had often played mixed hockey on the beach at a resort in Caernarvon-shire, not far from Bangor. He then went away again, and there was more discussion, after which they decided to accept my offer. The Comtesse was a spectator, and sweetly offered to look after my overcoat during the match.

Bad luck dogged me. Almost as soon as the game started, something must have gone wrong with one of my skates, for I slipped, staggered and fell heavily, tripping up two of our team, who had started a fine run. I apologized, but we lost a goal through it. Later, owing to my cold hands, my stick slipped out of my hand, and hit a member of the opposing side on the knee. He made rather a fuss, and later, when I hit our captain in the face – by accident, of course – with the ball, I was asked if I minded going off the field. I said, "One must always play for the good of one's side," and I quoted that thing by Kipling, "It isn't the player of the game that counts. It's the game."

So I went off and joined Germaine. In searching my overcoat for my brandy-flask, to stave off the cold, I discovered that I had lost it, which is most annoying. It was given to me by an admiral who knew my father. Such is life.

Yours ever,
O. THAKE

P.S. Tell Saunders to send out a lot of pearl studs. I keep mislaying mine.

Hotel Albernheit
St. Moritz

Really! I am very much worried, almost to the breaking point, at what's going on. Everything is disappearing. Even my clothes are beginning to go, and last night I found myself standing in my dress clothes, without a tail-coat to put on – mere shirt-sleeves. I cannot understand it at all. The Comtesse points out that there is a well-known conjurer staying in the hotel, but I tell her in reply, that we are not living in the Middle Ages of Black Magic, and anyhow, conjurers only take rabbits and watches. I cannot suspect the maids. What good would tailcoats be to them? I hardly know which way to turn. Meanwhile, will you tell Saunders to replenish my wardrobe as much as he can? I want him to send out a Thermos flask, some more cough mixture, a stamp album, and an alpenstock, all of which are missing.

I continue to play at cards, and to lose. Germaine partners me at bridge when we play with friends of hers, a Count Stanis – something or other, and his wife, and when I bid one no-trump, she never calls less than three or four. What a woman of spirit! What verve! What a flair, eh? Our eight hundred and fifty points down on one hand recently seemed nothing as a price to pay for her company.

Yours ever,
O. THAKE

Hotel Albernheit
St. Moritz

There is a very nice man here, who knows Russia inside out. I naturally asked him if he knew of the Tchavdnik mines, owned by the Comtesse. He said he could not recall the name.

"Anyhow," I told him, "I have shares in them, and they are bound to go up, because all the peasants need ore."

He replied, "Who stuffed you with all that nonsense? What on earth do you think the peasants would want with ore?"

To which I retorted, "Kindly remember you are criticizing a friend of mine. Besides, I am told from reliable sources that ore is essential out there."

He then said he didn't believe the mine existed at all, so I said, "There is no arguing with some people."

By the way, I have found a gold pencil-case that I had lost. The Comtesse was using it yesterday, and when I came up to her, in some surprise, she said, "I always return what I borrow. Just let me finish this note." I had forgotten I had ever lent her the thing, but what could I do but make her a present of it?

I must apologize for troubling Saunders so much. Apparently I had lent her my gold fountain-pen as well. I have given her that too, as well.

Yesterday an unfortunate thing happened. We were playing bridge, Germaine and I against the Count and his wife. We lost rather heavily, and I, of course, offered to pay the whole thing. I produced the notes and asked the Count for a hundred francs change – which I mislaid. These continual losses are most annoying. Still, one cannot have everything in this life.

Yours ever,
O . THAKE

Hotel Albernheit
St. Moritz

I wonder who it was who said, "Life has thorns, but it also has roses." It is very true, and the roses make the thorns worthwhile, too. Last night, Germaine and I went for a stroll after dinner, and something in the atmosphere made me reckless. I took her arm, and said, "Can you not hear a thousand nightingales?"

"*Ma foi!* No," said she. "They do not sing in this weather."

"I mean in the imagination," said I.

"My friend," she answered, "I cannot tell what it is goes on in your imagination, can I?"

I laid my hand on her arm.

"When the heart speaks," I said, "one understands."

"What does speak your heart?" she asked.

"Could I but tell you," I rejoined, "the very leaves should drop from their branches."

And so under the throbbing sky, we chatted.

Were she not so fresh and innocent, so unused to the world's harshness, I should have taken her in my arms there and then. But what right had I, all stained with experience and travel, to presume to pluck this wayside cottage bloom? The mind revolts at the thought. So I merely stroked her ear, and said, "One day, little thing, when life has opened your eyes, you will understand."

And she said, "Ah, I know so little bit. Sometimes I long to understand all things. But even to a fresh little girl like I come lovely surprise and rewards."

She pressed close to me, and for a second the stars held their breath. I was a king. I could have ridden out, and shot a dragon.

The moment passed. We found ourselves in a village. We took a motor-car home, but I found I had lost all my money. She, with that generosity that makes her a Helen, a Florence Nightingale, lent me the fare.

As we came into the hotel, a strange man spoke to her abruptly. I could have flogged him, but she disarmed me with a sweet smile.

Yours truly,
O.THAKE

P.S. Tell Saunders to stop sending me tomatoes. I have not lost any, and even if I had, could replace them.

Hotel Albernheit
St. Moritz

I do not like the look of things. There is something suspicious about the Comtesse. Not, of course, that I suspect her of anything – I would sooner suspect an Empress. But all day today she has seemed uneasy, and a number of strange men have been asking for her. One or two of them questioned me, and I said, "She is on the top of a very high mountain ski-ing, and will not be down for a day or two." They asked me if I had missed any personal belongings lately. I said, "Yes, a lot. Has she also then?" To which they answered, "No, no. Quite the reverse. She's missed nothing, apparently."

"Ah," I said, "I am glad to hear that."

When I told her all this, she seemed very much worried, but I took her hand and swore that all should be well. She asked what the men looked like, and I, to cheer her up, said, "Oh, funny looking fellows, with bowlers, like the detectives in plays."

She then became sentimental, and spoke of having to leave hurriedly, on account of an illness in Suffolk.

As we sat talking, two men entered the room, without knocking. She hid behind me in fear, and I guessed they meant harm to her.

"Where is the Comtesse?" asked one of them.

"In Suffolk," I shouted, "at least, packing to go there."

"Come out of it," said the second man, catching sight of her head under my elbow. The Comtesse rose superbly.

"Aggie Carter," said the first man, "you are wanted. Better come quietly."

"Strike me pink, you again, Bob," she answered, without a trace of French accent.

Then I guessed she was playing a part to get rid of them. So I supported her by crying, "An' strike me bloomin' pink, too, guv'nor."

But nobody took any notice, and out she went, laughing, with the two men. I don't know what it all can mean. I hope it will be cleared up when I next write.

Yours ever,
O. THAKE

How horrible is this world when stripped of all its romance! How ungrateful is man! How base is woman! Even a countess of the blood, can, it seems, crawl lower than the beasts of the field – for I still believe her, in some way, to be what she seemed.

Hardly had I recovered from the surprise of seeing her go off with these men, when a third appeared, and motioned me to follow him. He took me into her boudoir, flung open a cupboard, and showed me all my missing property – coats, studs, links, money, pencils, watches, and so on.

"You will, of course, charge her," he said.

"How do I know who put them there?" I countered. "It might have been you."

This he called a foolish suggestion, and he went on to explain how my letters, published in the *Daily Express*, had put Scotland Yard on the track of the notorious Aggie Carter, alias Sonia Tumbelova, alias Mitzi Grunenwald. "She always takes a different name," he said, "and she always does her job by vamping. That's why we sent men out here to investigate. She usually works with Red Pete."

Judge of my surprise and indignation. It was I, I who had brought this on her, by my babbling letters, I who had stirred the Yard to action. How was I to make amends?

"You are all wrong," I said to the man. "There has been some mistake. Red Pete is nothing to me, and I never yet heard of Aggie Carter. Take care you do not miscarry justice, and arrest an innocent girl. I shall not prefer a charge."

"That's as you please, sir," he said, "she's wanted for lots of things, and we have a warrant."

"What's she wanted for, as you call it?" I inquired sarcastically.

"Forgery, sir, shoplifting, housebreaking . . ."

"It is preposterous," I said, "and she will explain. Take me to her. Let me see the Comtesse."

In my next letter I will describe what followed, and my farewell interview with her, who to me is still Comtesse Germaine Eulalie Nicolette Cécile de Mont-Saint-Brignolles-le-Vaurien.

Yours ever,
O. THAKE

P.S. Tell Saunders this is no time to send me apples that squeak when you pinch them. Is he insane?

Hotel Albernheit
St. Moritz

She has gone. No more shall I hear her voice on the sofa. They have taken her away, like a cast-off glove. I got permission to see her once more, and she, in her bravery, was laughing. When I said, "You are the Comtesse. Tell them they lie in their teeth," she replied, "You big stiff! You bonehead! You boob! I'm Aggie Carter."

So I said, "Madam, you may be Aggie Smith even, but to me you will never be aught but the Comtesse." And I bowed.

"Coo!" she said. "Hark at George. Gee up, little Lord Fauntleroy!"

"Madam," said I, "I do not know the peer to whom you refer, nor is my name George, but I forgive you for these levities, even as I do for your graver misdemeanours. You have taken advantage of my passion. Be that as it may, I thank you for the happy hours you have given me. They were worth anything else that may have happened. I trust I am honourable enough to forget the latter, and remember the former. So long as I bear the name of Thake, chivalry shall not suffer. Madame la Comtesse Germaine Eulalie Nicolette Cécile de Mont-Saint-Brignolles-le-Vaurien, I bid you good-bye. The incident is closed. I thank you."

She then said, "I can't do it," and gave me back a gold fountain-pen she had apparently just taken playfully from my waistcoat pocket. Then she laughed again, and shouting, "Cheero, sugar-daddy!" vanished through the door, like a rose that flutters to the ground.

Sugar-daddy! And I had visions of the French lovers' phrases she would use to me. Sugar-daddy! Really! Oh! Germaine! Germaine! Germaine! Were you a dream?

Yours,
O. THAKE

It may be noticed that whenever Mr Thake is deeply moved, he expresses his feelings in poetry. He is evidently deeply moved at the present time, for I have just come across these verses in the Engadine Herald:

ALONE
BY AUDAX

High and far above my head
    The snow-capped peaks in silence stand,
The sunset glows a glorious red,
    And here in the gathering dusk I stand.

The night wind softly blows along,
    And darker grow the gigantic rocks,
The stars will peep out ere long,
    With all their shining golden locks.

Ah, what is this deep pang I feel?
  My bosom heaves, my throat is dry,
And no longer may I conceal
  The fact that I could almost cry.

Draw near, sweet presence, soothe my woe
  With touches of that gentle hand,
And then this Alpine world below
  Shall once more be smiling and bland.

Ah, goddess of the winking mirth,
  Draw near once more to my lone heart,
I am the wretchedest man on earth
  When you and I are kept apart.

❖ XI ❖

Paris

LATEST ARRIVALS

Hotel Barnsley: *Colonel and Mrs Edward Rabbit, Sir Walter Mainwopple, Mr Oswald Thake, Miss Shovel, Mrs Utter and Miss Desdemona Utter, Herr Hugo Schwarnheit, the Hon. Mrs Fudge and Master Eric Fudge, Mrs Nargle and family, Captain Fowlhouse, Miss Nodd, Rear-Admiral Sir Arthur Anymore, Lady Ough, Mr Forbes-Melon, Miss Netta Forbes-Melon, Mr Ulyate A. Niceman and Miss Sukie A. Niceman, Senator Rowle, Mrs Grist, and Mlle Rose Duchanel.*

Hotel Barnsley
Paris

MY DEAR BEACHCOMBER,

The pleasure with which I take up my pen to write to you again, has been a little marred by an unhappy incident. As you will see, I am staying at the Barnsley, where Tom Watson always comes – and Mrs Staines too, with her cousin – you remember Gallop who used to play the cello after tea. Well, I arrived here yesterday, and at the same moment as my taxi – if they call them that here – drove up, another drove up from the other direction. I got out, taking no notice, and out of the other descended a young woman, obviously French, as she spoke French to the man. She was behind me when I reached the hotel door, so I stopped, and with an "*Après vous,*" meaning "After you," I motioned her to precede me, which she did. We thus came into the vestibule together, and the manager came forward and spoke to us. I don't know what he said, but the young woman frowned, and moved away from me, and then the manager said to me in English, "I beg your pardon for the mistake. I thought you were with this lady." I interrupted him angrily, and said I had never even seen her before, and explained that I had only said "After you," to her.

I then got into the lift, and found the young woman in it. She turned her back on me. I said, wishing to show that it wasn't my fault, "*Pardon, madame où mademoiselle.*" But she only said very loudly something ending with a word like "insupportable".

I was perturbed to discover that our rooms were on the same floor, and the baggage-man led us along a passage. He showed the young woman into room No. 42, and put my baggage into No. 43 – the next room. This was too much, so risking English, I turned to the young woman as she entered her room, and said, "Madam, I can't help it. They have allotted us adjoining rooms, but it is no design of mine." I got no further, for she slammed the door in my face, and I tripped over a mat just as the man came by. He laughed very much at my predicament, I don't know why.

I shall start exploring Paris tomorrow.

Yours ever,
O . THAKE

P.S. Tell Saunders to get me a map with the River Seine marked on it clearly, and send it out here.

Hotel Barnsley
Paris

I flatter myself that I am pretty quick on the uptake, and I think I shall soon have Paris sized up. Already I am picking up phrases rapidly, although everybody here talks English. This morning I asked for a typical French breakfast, and the waiter smiled and said, "How you English joke always!" I said, "It is no joke.

While I am in Paris I wish to do as Paris does, out of compliment to a great nation and one that did much to save civilization in the Great War. Entente Cordiale, monsieur. Vive!" The waiter said he was sorry, but people always had bacon and eggs for breakfast. I said, "But not the French?" and he said not many French ever came there, which seems odd to me. Perhaps that's why the hotel is called the "Barnsley". I don't know, though.

Paris is very gay. And although it is not as big as London it seems quite big. London certainly has no Eiffel Tower, but then Paris has no Albert Memorial. It cuts both ways, and there are not as many streets in the French capital. Of course, one hears French spoken on every side, which adds to the strangeness, and the traffic keeps to the right instead of to the left, the result being that a vehicle, whichever way it is going is on the opposite side to the one it would be on if it were in England, even when it is going in the reverse direction. The police have a foreign look about them, probably because one expects the English helmet.

The people are very quick-witted. I went into a shop to buy some views, and before I spoke the assistant said in English, "A view of the Opera, sir?" I said, "How did you know I was English?" and the assistant shrugged her shoulders. Then two Americans came in, and she guessed them too – but she was obviously helped by hearing one of them say Paris was a nifty burg, whatever that barbarous term may connote.

I am getting quite what they call the *Joie de vive*.

Yours ever,
O. THAKE

P.S. Ask Saunders what on earth use he thinks it is to send me a map of Europe, with Spain underlined in red ink. I said the Seine. Spain, tell him, is not a river, much less is it in Paris.

I think I may say, without exaggeration, that I am now part of the seething life of the Boulevard. I am at this moment sipping an *apéritif* at a café table as I write to you. At the same table is an Englishman named Robinson, with whom I have struck up an acquaintance. He is some sort of an authority on leather, and talks very interestingly of it, and he tells me that his son by his first marriage has just come back from a big game-hunting expedition, which he had been asked to join – in the same way as Wentworth last year, curiously enough. It is meeting people in this way that makes one realize how travel opens the mind. After all, there is nothing like conversation to bring one to a fuller knowledge of one's fellow beings – or, for that matter, *vice versa* – I mean to bring one's fellow beings to a fuller knowledge of oneself.

I can't make women out. The lady who arrived here when I did, and occupies the room next to mine, came into the lounge here yesterday and smiled. I rose and bowed, and was beginning to speak, when a man who had been behind me stepped forward and greeted her. He was apparently an old friend who had called for her, and it was at him, not me, she smiled. Well, once more I tried to apologize, but she simply turned her back and walked off with him. I don't know why I should always be doomed like this.

Robinson tells me that the really typical French quarter here is the upper end of the Rue de Rivoli and the Rue St. Honoré, so I am going there today.

Yours ever,
O. THAKE

P.S. There are times when Saunders seems to be demented. Why, for instance, should he send me a tuning-fork, when I ask for a map of the River Seine? I shall end by buying the map here. And if everybody did that what would become of British goods?

Yesterday Mr Robinson – who, I have discovered, has a cousin living in Stockport, where Tom used to go – or was it Birmingham? Anyhow, we went to a restaurant called *Chez Wilkins*, which is apparently *the* smart place to lunch, or *déjeuner*, as they say here. It's an English name, but typically French in atmosphere. Robinson pointed out to me how many English and Americans go there, on that account. He then took me to the old palace of the Louvre, which is now a big shop, and showed me a large equestrian statue of General Sarrail outside the cathedral. I bought a rather neat ash-tray for Mrs Watson, with "A present from Gay Paris," written on it in English, and a china mug for her boy, with a picture on it of the Bourse or Stock Exchange, during a snowfall, and the words, "Souvenir of the Gay City." The attendant asked me if I was American, and I said, "No. The next best thing," at which we both laughed with that spirit of *camaraderie* and *bonhomie* that makes the *Entente* a living thing. Here was I, an English exile, and he a native Frenchman, brought together for a moment by fate, and yet both able to appreciate the same jest. A most impressive thought!

In the evening I went off alone to see a play, but as I could not understand much of it, I left and went on to a sort of revue instead. Really! I don't know if these people have a Lord Chamberlain to keep them decent, but I should imagine not. It made me glad I was alone. Suppose, for instance, old Miss Cail

157

or Mrs Ranter had been with me. I say decisively that these French revues are not the kind of show to which one would care to take one's friends. Yet I stayed it out, chiefly because of the remarkable performance of an actress for whom I prophesy a great future. I kept the programme, so that I can watch her progress until she becomes a star. Her name is Mistinguett.

I must go to the well-known Moulin Rouge, or one of those places soon.

Yours ever,
O. THAKE

Hotel Barnsley
Paris

I have been to a sort of cabaret show at the *Lapin Qui Murmure*, and I must say that it has taken my breath away. Really! No sooner had I paid for my ticket and walked in, than a man said, in bad English, too:

"That will be ten francs."

I replied, "What will?"

He then repeated, "Ten francs, please," and I said, "I have paid for my ticket."

"That," he said, "is different."

"What is different from what?" I asked – not unreasonably, I think.

"That," he said, "was for the ticket. This is an entrance fee for dancing."

I told him I did not intend to dance, and he said it was twenty francs to look on. So I paid up and sat down at a table.

A waiter came up and said, "That will be forty francs."

"What will?" I asked, my anger rising in my gorge.

"The champagne," said he, pointing to a bottle already on the table.

"I didn't order it," said I.

"That," he said, "is as Monsieur wills."

Whereupon he took it away, brought me some lemonade and a siphon, and asked for thirty-five francs. Sheer robbery, I call it. After that a man came up and charged me twenty francs for the cabaret.

"When is it?" I asked.

"It is over," he said, "Monsieur was late."

It occurred to me later that I might as well have champagne. So I had it. After I had drunk a good deal of that typical wine I enjoyed the cabaret, particularly a song that had a chorus of "Ya-Ya-Ya-Ya". One had to pay forty francs to stay for this second cabaret and another sixty as a *pourboire* for the commissionaire, who told me it was customary to give the head waiter one hundred francs. The head waiter said everyone gave the cloakroom man eighty francs, and the cloakroom man told me I ought to give the other commissionaire fifty francs. Then a programme seller claimed thirty francs and told me I ought to give the wine waiter fifty francs. I gave the wine waiter's assistant fifty francs, and he hinted that I ought to give another assistant sixty francs, so I gave all the waiters fifty francs, and another commissionaire, who said he was keeping a cab for me, asked for eighty francs, and I gave the boy at the door a hundred.

It is all a trifle scandalous, but what would you, in Paris?

Yours ever,
O . T H A K E

P.S. Saunders seems to me to have been odd from birth onwards.

I cannot write much today, as I am exceedingly worried. On returning from the cabaret show of which I told you, at the *Lapin Qui Murmure*, I made my way to the hotel. The lady with whom I always seem to be involved here, drove up in a car just after me. As I held the door open for her, a champagne bottle dropped from my overcoat pocket on to the pavement. It smashed and covered her feet with the dregs of the wine. Some malignant fairy must have put the bottle in my pocket. I was speechless with shame, and could only try to wipe her feet with my handkerchief. But she thrust me aside angrily – and my fear is that she will complain to the proprietor of the Barnsley. If she does, it looks so odd. How can I explain?

I am in a great perturbation of mind.

Yours ever,
O. THAKE

As I expected, the worst has happened. The proprietor of the Barnsley, M. Pultzheim, sent for me yesterday, and referred to the unfortunate incident of my dropping the champagne bottle. The lady apparently complained very strongly to him, and said that I dogged her footsteps wherever she went. I told him that I resented the implication, and had no intention of dogging at all. He then asked me how I came to be walking about at two in the morning dropping champagne bottles outside a respectable hotel and drenching ladies' feet in liquor. I retorted with heat that I was not walking but riding, and that it wasn't two but two-thirty, that I only dropped *one* bottle outside *one* hotel, and only *one* foot was drenched, and champagne is hardly liquor. All this seemed to make no impression on him, so I said it all again slowly. He said the lady insisted on an apology. Really! As if I hadn't tried to make one!

I think I shall move to another hotel. They all whisper and giggle here when I enter a room, and a gross American came up to me a short while ago, winked both eyes, slapped my back, and said, "Bully for the lads of the village!"

"Lads of what village?" I inquired coldly.

"No flies on you," said he.

"I should sincerely hope there are not," said I.

"Bottles are sure slippery things after midnight," he said.

"Maybe," I replied. "Maybe not."

I seem to remember that the Hoopoes used to stay at an hotel called the Hotel Malsain. I must ask about it, especially as the American keeps on winking at me, and even brought his wife up and said:

"Sadie, this is the guy that worked the bottle stuff on the jane."

And his wife said, "My, mister, glad to meet you."

What is one to do? And all because some demon put that bottle in my overcoat pocket.

Yours ever,
O. THAKE

I have moved to the Hotel Malsain, but by some misfortune, I seem to have got somebody else's luggage. I don't recognize the trunks at all, and there's a lady's travelling case. By the way, I need not have moved here at all, as the lady with whom I became so involved was leaving also, on the same day. I haven't attempted to unpack these trunks until I can get some explanation.

The proprietor of the Barnsley, in a grossly insulting and insinuating manner, accuses me by telephone of going off with his guest's luggage. Really! I told him his own clumsy servants put this into the cab without consulting me . . .

It now appears that it is her luggage I have got, and she has been making a great fuss because they put mine in her taxi. Shall I never get rid of all this nonsense and humbug? Her maid has been round here, and she jabbered and flicked her fingers at me and shouted French until I didn't know whether I was on my head or my heels, and didn't care either. I don't know what names the maid called me, but all the servants laughed, so I suppose they were funny ones.

The strain of Paris is beginning to tell on me. I wonder why I ever came.

Yours ever,
O. THAKE

Confusion worse confounded upon confusion! The proprietor of the Barnsley, M. Pultzheim, came round yesterday with the French lady and her maid. There was a dreadful scene. The lady blamed me, and he blamed me, and I could only follow a word here and there. However, I gave up the luggage, and received in exchange a lot of boxes labelled Stapleworth. When I attempted to point out that they were not mine, all three of them turned on me and said I was trying to complicate matters. Then an American came in, shouting out that he wouldn't stand for it. "I am Cyrus Q. Stapleworth, of Themistocles, Neb.," he said, "and I say it is a frame-up." The place became a pandemonium until a man called Beetham arrived with my luggage and claimed his own. "Am I a furniture department?" I queried. "Am I a luggage office, ladies and gentlemen?"

Nobody answered, but they all went out fighting.

I am worn out.

Yours ever,
O. THAKE

I have met here a most intelligent young writer. He took me last night after dinner to a café in the Latin Quarter where the poet Saprelotte used to sit and drink with his friends. I expected to find a place like the Cheshire Cheese, but was disappointed. Apparently, the proprietor of the place had not even kept Saprelotte's glass or his fork, and there are no portraits of him there. My friend, whose name is Wood, explained that Saprelotte was the first poet to write poems that had to be printed in the shape of liqueur glasses – a most original trick – why have not our poets this enterprise? He founded a school, and they called themselves the Poopooists. I asked if Poopooism is still a force, and Wood said the Zutists had ousted it. The Zutists believe that all art is dynamic, and they write with squibs dipped in moist gunpowder. It is all very interesting. Wood himself told me that he lives in a bare attic, and rarely eats anything. However, he says that without his father's monthly allowance of five thousand francs he would be destitute, as these bare attics are very expensive now, and are let out by a firm that owns a lot of them.

I saw many picturesque people at this café, but was surprised to hear what they were. One man, with a beard and an open collar, who looked like a poet, was, Wood told me, a well-known bicyclist; and when I spotted what I took to be a lady artist, it turned out to be an American prohibition lecturer. Once a very pale young man in a broad-brimmed hat and baggy trousers got up and started to shout. They threw him out, and Wood informed me that he worked in an English bank in Paris, and sometimes took too much to drink. However, it is all most fascinating.

Yours ever,
O . THAKE

I spent most of yesterday in the Parisian Underground Railway, but through no fault of my own. I had intended to go and visit the Bastille, but I found that the Underground people, unlike those at the hotel, spoke only in French. I had left my phrase-book at the hotel, and so was rather helpless. The result was that I kept changing from one train to another, saying "Bastille". What the replies of the guards and other officials were, I cannot say, but I was considerably jostled. At the end of it all, I decided to stop it, as I was hungry, so I got out and found myself near the Eiffel Tower. Later on an Englishman told me that, anyhow, there was only the left wing of the Bastille left to see, so I didn't miss much.

We had a little music here after dinner in the hotel. One of the visitors, an English lady, who teaches in a school in Lancashire, brought out her violin, and her sister played the piano and occasionally sang. Out of compliment to the French guests and the staff, she played the "Marseillaise", and some of us joined in the chorus. After that all the French people left the room – some left even in the middle. They are an emotional people, and I suppose the associations were too poignant, and the whole thing too painful for them. Sensitiveness, whether in man or woman, Englishman or foreigner, is no discredit.

The sister was encored for a beautiful piece, called as I afterwards ascertained, "The Sailor's Vision". I must get Saunders to send it out to me. Then we had "O Sole Mio" on the violin, followed by "Scots Wha Hae". The evening was a great success. To wind up a man sang his old school song "Boys of Chelmcote, Steady and True". I wish the old Chelmcotians could have been there.

Yours ever,
O. THAKE

I have had an exceedingly interesting discussion on French history with an American business man, a Mr Gideon B. Schnell. I was saying how marvellous it was of the French to produce such a superman as Napoleon Bonaparte. But he said it had always been his opinion that Napoleon was overrated.

"He had a certain amount of goods," he said, "but he didn't sell 'em properly."

I asked him what he meant, and he said, "Just imagine what that man could have done if they'd turned him into a sort of company and syndicated him. He had a lot of pep, but he didn't have our modern efficiency urge. Salesmanship was what he lacked. He shouldn't have wasted so much time fighting."

"But," said I, "if he'd been in business, the English would never have had their Waterloo."

To which he replied that you don't have to go to war to win a Waterloo, and handed me a leaflet all about himself, and Schnell's Health Tablets, and how two of them kill any disease.

"That's my Waterloo," he said, "and I don't need no grand army."

I have been to the Quai d'Orsay, where, I am told, the guillotine used to stand. And it is a solemn thought that here the revolutionaries swarmed round the scaffold uttering fierce, bloodthirsty yells, against the defenceless duchesses and marchionesses. That, I think, will ever be a blot on the French character, and it only shows to what lengths an ill-educated mob will go unless controlled by the iron hand of state discipline. Not even a royal head is safe, and the ante-rooms of palaces become the hog-pens of the masses. Thus, at any rate, I read the lesson of French history.

I have visited the Opera, but it was all in French and Italian. I noticed that hardly anyone wore evening dress – a national laxity I deplore. But I am thankful to say that whenever I saw the welcome sight of a man or woman fittingly attired, they turned out to be my own countrymen. This kind of thing makes one proud of the Flag.

Yours ever,
O. THAKE

Hotel Malsain
Paris

I have been observing the French traffic. After the restful methods employed in our own English streets, Paris is exceedingly nerve-racking. What I mean is that the police do not interfere often enough with the vehicles, and when they do, it is only for a very short time, all of which must make great demands on the nerves of the French. Those long pauses to which we are accustomed, and which help one to recuperate from shocks and accidents, are unknown here. Of course, you get to your destination quicker, but at what a price!

The French also drink whenever they like – a dangerous and demoralizing habit. Only yesterday, an Englishman with whom I was taking a Dubonnet and soda, said wistfully, "How one misses the cheery 'Time please, gentlemen,' of our own places of refreshment. I am homesick, I declare, for the cheery smile which accompanies this remark, as your glass is efficiently whipped away in a trice, almost before you are aware the Great Machine is at work." And then he added some remarkable sentences, spoken like an economist. "Loitering over drink," he said, "takes valuable hours off the working day, and valuable hours off the working day lose the world's markets. Sooner or later, the social structure breaks. Mark my words, France is doomed."

The Arc de Triomphe is most imposing. I am told it was built from the guns taken during Napoleon's Russian campaign. Remarkable!

Yours ever,
O . THAKE

Hotel Malsain
Paris

Yesterday I discovered a very pleasant little café in the Place Pigalle, where there was music. A young man sang a song of his own, and then sold copies of it. I bought one, but I doubt if I shall ever sing it. Then a girl danced – and she threw me a rose – a paper one, of course. It went into my coffee, but I pulled it out as gallantly as I could, dried it on my handkerchief, and asked the waiter to give it back to her. This seemed to annoy her at first, but afterwards she laughed, and spoke to a party at a table near her. They laughed, and everybody looked at me in a spirit of the nicest *camaraderie*. I felt quite proud. After that, the girl singled me out and shouted, "You do not like roses, *hein*?" I replied that, after daffodils, they were my favourite blooms, and there was more friendly laughter.

Later I passed a weird-looking place, that looked like one of the wicked places one hears about. I went in – in all innocence, of course – and found a number of men and women sitting in rows. They were listening to a pale tall man with a beard, who was standing up in front of them, and reading from a small book. From his sad voice I gathered that he was reading poetry. I listened for about half an hour, but could not understand it. I suppose it was decadent poetry. Just as I was going, an ill-looking man held a plate towards me for money, and offered me a book of poetry, which I bought. It was called "Tristesse d'Antan", which I suppose is the heroine's name.

Yours ever,
O. THAKE

Hotel Malsain
Paris

On the eve of leaving the "gay city" it occurs to me that a few original observations may interest you – together with my conclusions as to matters French – and therefore Parisian.

Paris, though smaller, of necessity, than London, nevertheless conveys an impression of size, but she lacks somehow, what I call striking buildings. There is nothing like the Crystal Palace. Again, her monuments are less original. It is true there is a column rather like the Nelson Column, but no figure surmounts it. The French love gaiety, and they drink more wine than we do. They talk faster – (but I must be fair. Tom Watson discovered that long before I did, and told me to expect it). Paris has less railway stations of importance, and fewer theatres. So you see, in all the ingredients of civilization she is behind us – since talking fast and drinking wine need not necessarily be accounted virtues or accomplishments worthy of pride.

They have made me very comfortable at the Hotel Malsain, and I only go because a shadow from the unhappy past has brushed me with gentle wing. As I walked yesterday in the Bois de Boulogne a motor-car passed close to me. In it, surrounded by all the accompaniments of wealth and leisure, and escorted by a grey-bearded man, sat, or rather reclined, her whose very name once imparted a kick to my pulse and brought a mist before my eyes. I stood as one transfixed. Her eyes met mine, but in them I read no recognition. I was forgotten, like last year's clothes.

For this reason, my dear Beachcomber, rather than open old wounds, I take my leave of the gay city of Paris – not wishing it ill, but rather as one flying from peril. You shall hear from me again, when I have laid this ghost. Dear me, dear me, the power of affection in middle life!

Yours ever,
O. THAKE

✦ XII ✦

IRMA DE POURBOIRE

My Dear Beachcomber,

I take up my pen once more to write to you, as one who may possibly interest you in a project. My sojourn at this fashionable resort, which shall be nameless for the present – not that my mentioning it would add to its lustre – I am not vain enough, I hope, to imagine that – has brought me into daily, nay, well-nigh hourly contact with those whose faces are household words in our Press. Though I am not necessarily on speaking terms with them all, I cannot but observe how they conduct themselves – I mean nothing detrimental or derogatory.

It therefore occurs to me that the papers often print paragraphs and notes about people – mostly, apparently, the intimate friends of the writer. And since your readers used to be interested in my letters, I thought I might do something of the sort for you, accompanied by snapshots or sketches. I would, of course, take care not to expose you to libel actions by any indiscretion on my part, and I thought you might give my notes some good, catchy, journalistic heading such as, "Some First-Hand Observations of Many People and Things at a Fashionable Holiday Resort from Day to Day – by the Gentleman Who is on the Spot Nearly All the Time". But I leave the title to you. That is only a suggestion thrown out, you know.

I may mention that I recently was in person the recipient of a correspondence course in literary journalism – six lessons in all, so that I do not bring to my *devoir* anything akin to the pen of a novitiate. This I tell you that you may preface my notes by telling the public that they are the work of one who has been initiated into the arcana of the trade, and not an inexperienced Pharisee, or perhaps I should say vandal?

Yours as ever,
O. Thake

The foregoing letter, both by its style and its matter, convinces me that I should be foolish not to take advantage of my friend's sugges-tion. The correspondence course has certainly had an effect on his style, and I have no doubt of his ability to make his notes readable. I have, therefore, accepted his suggestion, and asked him to start sending me material as soon as he can. His title I find rather clumsy for daily journalism. Instead, I suggest "Here and Now," over the signature of "The Man on the Spot."

DEAR BEACHCOMBER,

I note with pleasure that you intend to adopt my suggestion, but I would like to make a further remark on the subject. "Here and Now" is a shorter title than mine, but I doubt if it makes such an appeal. Also, I would rather you signed my notes with my own name than called me "The Man on the Spot". You see, the latter might suggest to the ignorant, that I was here specially as a professional to do this work – which would be derogatory and a lie. Journalism is only a side-line with me, and were I to be suspected of professionalism, I should be inundated with de-mands for work.

I saw Tom yesterday – but I am forgetting; I must keep that kind of *pièce de résistance* for my notes, must I not? No good spoiling the market for a ha'porth of tar, eh? But forgive me jesting. I mean to do the work seriously, and already I have a "scoop" in mind – a certain lady has arrived – mum's the word. You understand. Title and all that. You wait. Nor is that the only title here.

Of course, nobody here will know that I am a journalistic contributor, as I am not going to dress like one, and I flatter myself that those whom I interview will not know that they are being interviewed. I've got a book about that, full of useful hints. I might sometimes strike a more serious note in my notes –

forgive the pun! – such as Geneva, upon which I have decided opinions. How can you have peace unless you disarm? But there I go again. Well, well. I must go now and prepare my first instalment for you, and I think I can promise a sensation.

Yours truly,
O. THAKE

P.S. Tell Saunders to have my large camera sent out to me.

Mr Thake has sent his first paragraphs. I have not sub-edited them at all, but I have been at some pains to determine the cause of his curiously stilted style. Apparently his course of literary journalism is responsible for the repetition of "one", and for the editorial "we". The dashes, I imagine, are due to his efforts to avoid libel actions. They give one a sense of security, but at the same time, detract from the interest of the notes. I confess that I cannot begin to understand the photograph.

I have asked Mr Thake to make his style more human.

HERE AND NOW

One rises early here and takes one's bath, and has breakfast at one's leisure. At breakfast today one noticed Lady ___ , the Hon. Mrs ___ , Lord ___ , ___ the jockey, and Lady ___ . They all looked very well, I thought, and were eating one's breakfast.

On leaving one's hotel, I ran into one's old friend, Tom Watson, who is here. "Good morning, Thake," he said to us, and one answered, "Cheer-oh, Tom." One finds this *camaraderie* very gratifying, especially as it is entirely gratuitous. We think it is about time the Government should do something about mice in bathing-cabins, and we have consistently pointed out that only by dealing directly with the primary cause will immunity from these rodents be established.

It looks like rain as one writes.

It is raining as we write.

One publishes here a snapshot of Colonel ___ , taken during the siesta hour.

O. THAKE

I publish below Mr Thake's second contribution. He appears to have taken to heart my criticism of his stilted style, and the change is obvious. He also asks me to state that the photograph published yesterday was not of Colonel ___ , but of Lady ___ , and begs me to apologize on his behalf to both parties. He says in his letter, "I thought you desired a dignified commentary upon events, but I will endeavour to cultivate a more jaunty style. Tell me if it is more suitable."

The result of his efforts appears to be a curious mixture of several types of writing.

HERE AND NOW

"What-ho!" I said to a celebrated beauty yesterday, as she was about to enter the briny. Later I drank a cocktail with her, and she told me that she intends to sell her bees, as the intermittent buzzing annoys her. "Does it remind you of the telephone?" I hazarded. "No," she countered – the witty little vixen! – "But it gives me a *mal-de-tête*."

You never saw such tanned faces in your life. A well-known peer has christened our hotel the Tannery. He can balance an apple on his nose for two minutes. ___ calls him William Tell, and ___ the novelist who travels about with his own brand of tea, swears he will put that joke into his next. Thumbs up! Good for him! Tally-ho!

M'yes. One sees simply too, too exquisite robes here, and the dinkiest creations rub shoulders with the cutest bathing hats imaginable. The snapshot is of Lady ___ and friend. What about it? A winner, I think.

Lady ___ 's dog ___ , fell into the sea yesterday after drinking a saucer of champagne. A publisher, clad as he was, in fencing shorts and a zephyr, plunged in and rescued him. He laughingly demanded a reward, and Lady ___ , sporty as ever, threw him a bone. Whereupon, the incensed dog bit him in the left calf. "Half-calf," cried Lord ___ . "Now you'll need a new binding!"

Must say tootle-too till tomorrow, my old haricots. There may be no flies on this place, but there are plenty of mosquitoes. So cheerio, and hoping this finds you as it leaves me, in the pink (bathing-suit). I should worry!

O. THAKE

I wired to Mr Thake yesterday, pointing out that he appeared to be losing all restraint, and imploring him not to make his notes so American in tone. I also told him that as long as he uses his discretion he may tell us the names of the people he writes about, instead of putting dashes all the time. I received a most excited reply, saying that he had, after great pains, secured a most important and exclusive interview with Lady Cabstanleigh, in which several startling revelations were made. I print the interview as it stands. Mr Thake has evidently tried very hard.

STARTLING REVELATIONS OF A PEERESS

I found Lady Cabstanleigh in her well-appointed bijou villa by the blue Mediterranean. As I was shown in, she said, "I was afraid it was another of those dreadful reporters. How one hates publicity, Mr Thake! Between friends, I can tell you that I would rather die than be interviewed."

I smiled knowingly.

"Tell me," I said, "will you be entertaining upon a lavish scale this season, when you return to your domicile in the metropolis?"

"I shall give some dances and parties," returned her ladyship graciously.

"And what," I continued, "is your favourite flower?"

"Naughty man!" she rejoined, wagging her large finger at me. "You mustn't give me flowers. I love daffodils more than anything on earth. When they are in season, of course."

"Of course," I assented.

"How old are you?" I vouchsafed.

"Wicked satirist," she cried making a little *moué*. "This is going too far. Anyhow, I'm younger than that hateful old harridan, Mrs Screaming, who's lunching with me all this week, and far younger than that selfish, ugly, neurotic Lady Farribole, whom I stay with so often. How I loathe her gawky daughter, and what a cad of a husband! Oh, what a crowd! You know," she added, lowering her shrill voice, "you know her father did time, and they say her uncle robbed his own till, and got his partner sacked for theft. Too bad! But they're a dirty crew."

"Do you know anything about Arabella Fauncewaters?" I queried.

"Nothing good," she ventured. "She wears a dyed wig. Her teeth are false. And she's a beastly little scandal-monger, always chattering and gossiping and destroying people's good names. Her father was a Welsh grocer, who funked the war."

I rose with a bow, and expressing the hope that we might meet again, left her. Hastening back to my hotel, I wrote down these revelations, which I am pleased to be able to place before the public.

O. THAKE

Below I reprint extracts from a few letters received on the subject of Mr Thake's indiscreet interview with Lady Cabstanleigh. His revelations have created such a turmoil that I felt myself bound to write and tell him that "Here and Now" must be discontinued, and that if he wishes to go on with journalism, he must keep clear of society gossip. His reply was that he had a most important "scoop," and he promises to disclose something of first-rate importance and interest in the near future. He assures me that there will be no question of libel this time.

DEAR MR BEACHCOMBER,

The attention of our client, Lady Cabstanleigh, has been called to an alleged interview granted by her to a Mr Thake, a journalist at present abroad. Our client instructs us to demand an explanation, failing which we shall be forced to take legal proceedings . . .

DEAR MR BEACHCOMBER,

So that old cat Cabstanleigh has been mewing again. I certainly do not intend to indulge in mutual recrimination, so I content myself with observing that she is an ill-natured, libellous, frowsy, conceited little backbiter, old enough to be my mother . . .

Lady Farribole notes that Lady Cabstanleigh has seen fit to discuss her with a low journalist, and to invent a tissue of lies about her. She has placed the matter in the hands of her solicitors . . .

And Mrs Fauncewaters asks me to state that, as her wig was made by the same firm as Lady Cabstanleigh's, her ladyship has nothing to crow about. Only half her teeth are false, and her father was not a Welsh grocer, but a Scotch one. To say that he avoided the war is a wicked lie. He was, for the whole duration, a kind of honorary batman to the Inspector of Veterinary Surgeons in the Isle of Wight, with the rank and pay of a lance-sergeant . . .

Mr Thake has apologized to the parties concerned. His latest letter to me says:—

. . . I should like it pointed out that, far from being a low "journalist," I am merely a novice, who, by getting exclusive information hitherto unpublished, seems to have embroiled the upper ten. I shall henceforth strike new pastures, conscious of the dignity of our profession, but proud of having published facts unknown to the public before. Let society rest in peace: it shall not hear from me again. If the cap has fitted, let those with guilty consciences wear it. Distinctions are invidious. I mention no names. The truth is never pleasant, and he who tells it gets more kicks than pence. The path of the pioneer is a lonely one, but it leads to the goal.

Tell Saunders to cross off all the titled names from the visiting list in the hall.

There is staying here in unassuming fashion an actress who, though at present obscure, is destined one day to set the welkin on fire. I have been privileged to meet her. Her name is Irma de Pourboire, but she is English, and a remote descendant of the Valois kings. Her name may have militated against her success. She tells me that she deals every day with scores of offers for film work and stage work. She was recently offered £500 a week to go to America – by an English manager in whose show she was playing – but she did not think the climate would suit her. He said he would make it Australia, but she was afraid of the natives and their boomerangs – very properly I think.

She says I may tell the readers of the *Daily Express* that she is twenty-one, and was educated at Cheltenham and Cambridge, her father being a cavalryman in India, and that she is nothing to do with the Pourboires who make soap-boilers near Coventry. She showed me her crest and her signet-ring, and sang "Crawlin' Along" for me. What a voice! Oh! Really! I asked her what parts she had played, and she made a mental calculation, but found it impossible to remember them all. One of her recent ones was Fifi in Pou-Pou, but she only had to cough off the stage in Act III, and so had little scope to show her mettle. She often takes small parts, out of eccentricity, she says.

Unfortunately, she is far from happy, and suffers from loneliness. Two men want to marry her, one a millionaire in the steel trade, and the other a banker, who has called his yacht Irma, after her. But she will not marry for money, or desert her art. Her indifference to money is beautiful, and sometimes she buys things in shops, and forgets to pay. Of course, I pay, but it is a little awkward when other people are in the shops. The other night she said she would give me a little dinner, so we went to the *Enorme*, which is the best restaurant here. She ordered a magnificent dinner, and the very best wines, and then found she had left her money at home. If that isn't the real Bohemian spirit, I don't know what is! I was delighted, and told her so, which, I flatter myself, seemed to please her. She smiled for the rest of the evening – but perhaps I delude myself. Really! How irresistible is charm, is it not?

I wonder who it was who spoke of "life going gaily as a marriage bell." I am enjoying myself immensely – not, of course, that I mean anything ulterior by the marriage bell simile. Far from it. I am a man built for the platonic relationship, and I seem to have a gift for drawing out the friendship in others. Irma de Pourboire says I have a genius for friendship, and that I have saved her from lonely boredom. What a little Bohemian – that is the word for her – she is – and yet not dirty and untidy like some. Her moods are extraordinary. Yesterday she again invited me to dinner. But just when we had finished our coffee and liqueurs, and the waiter was about to bring the bill, she jumped up and said she must go and look at the moon. And off she went. I admire a woman who can have her mind removed from the petty financial considerations of life all in a moment, like that.

"She is singular, mademoiselle," said the waiter. "There is no moon tonight."

Which is but one more evidence of her vague, romantic Bohemianism.

When she returned later, I told her there was no moon.

"No," she said, "but I can always imagine it up there in the sky, so remote, so lonely."

Isn't that beautiful?

She then opened her bag, and when I told her I had paid the bill during her absence, she became most annoyed, but forgave me later most graciously.

While I was in the casino with her, Tom Watson appeared, and whispered behind his hand, "Clicked again, Oswald?" or something equally vulgar. The man is impossible. I whispered back, "I do not know to what you may refer, but you are wide of the mark." He then made signs to me, until Irma asked me what was going on. I had to introduce them, and as he left later on, he muttered to me, "What a beauty!" I had to pretend he had spoken of my hat, and I replied aloud, "I got it in Paris." Whereupon the fool burst into loud laughter. It was most awkward. As though one couldn't get a hat in Paris!

It really is extraordinary that any actress of Irma's attainments should not be more widely known. Yesterday I happened to be taking tea with her, when the post was brought in. The very first letter she picked up, she told me, was from a manager, a famous manager, offering her a leading part in a new play. She just threw it down, and said the author wasn't good enough for her. The next letter asked her to star in a big film, but with a gesture of contempt she threw it aside, torn into a thousand fragments. "If they think I'll take an offer that's made to me in an envelope that looks like a bill, they're very wrong," she said angrily. "Fancy expecting me to lease a poky little theatre like –," she continued later, in reference to another letter.

"I wonder you don't employ a secretary," I said.

"That's not what I want," she replied. "What I want is a really good publicity man."

"Publicity man!" I cried. "Surely you cannot need that. You mean a man for propaganda."

"Of course that's what I mean," she said.

After a long pause, I said, "Of what kind?"

"An efficient one," she said. "I've had to sack four this year."

I suggested that I might try my hand, purely in an amateur way, as I had some journalistic experience. She leapt at the idea.

"Don't you edit the "Here and Now" column for the *Daily Express*?" she said.

"I did, and wrote it too," I answered.

"You'll do," she said.

Really! Well, anyhow, I shall have to do something about it. We have talked it over. She says people will like to read about her clothes and her favourite hobbies, and that I must repeat any good jokes she makes, and that if ever she is in an accident I must write all about it, and also if she has jewels stolen. It ought to be easy, and I am only too glad to do her a service. And she has shown me specimens of what her former agents wrote about her, so that I can get an idea of the style.

He who helps, however little, to bring genius into the lime-light, is doing a good work.

Yours truly,
O. THAKE

P.S. Tell Saunders I don't want any more leaflets about treacle. Surely he can keep them till I come home. Has he no sense? And tell him to get into touch with Sir Gerald du Maurier at once.

A well-known manager writes to complain that he has been subjected to considerable annoyance by the repeated calls of a Mr Saunders. This Mr Saunders claims to have come on behalf of a Mr Thake to arrange for the immediate engagement of a Miss Irma de Pourboire, described as "the famous young actress". The manager wishes to state that he has never heard of any of these three people.

I understand that other managers have been similarly troubled, and have received a ridiculous circular, addressed to the "Managers of Great Britain," and pointing out the necessity of recognizing genius.

Mr Thake appears to have lost no time in starting his new job as propagandist (the expression is his own) to Miss Irma de Pourboire. Today I opened a letter from him, and found inside it some typewritten sheets, from which I publish a few extracts:

. . . Irma de Pourboire, the brilliant and famous young actress is here. She intends to make a short stay here. Irma de Pourboire looks, I thought, very well. She will, of course, be heard of again soon in a big West End production.

. . . That young and famous actress, Irma de Pourboire, hopes to be seen shortly in a big West End play. When asked its name, Irma de Pourboire said it was at present a secret, but that it was a very big play with a leading part for Irma de Pourboire, that brilliant young actress.

. . . While walking on the beach here yesterday I noticed Irma de Pourboire, the celebrated stage star. She was talking to three earls and a viscountess. "Irma, dear, how well you look," said the second earl. "Yes, doesn't she?" said the viscountess! "Thumbs up!" retorted Irma de Pourboire, the renowned young genius, with a roguish grin.

. . . One of the most popular celebrities here is the famous young brilliant actress, Irma de Pourboire. There is a new cocktail called

Irma, and also a new dance called the Irma – in honour of Irma de Pourboire, the popular young actress.

. . . Irma de Pourboire, the famous young actress, whose favourite day of the week is Wednesday, has changed her favourite day to Tuesday, because of her narrow escape last Wednesday. Irma de Pourboire was driving along a coast road in her new car, when the two back wheels fell off. In her own words, "The car lurched, and I thought it was all up." But a handsome Marquis righted the machine, and Irma de Pourboire escaped with a shaking. She was wearing her famous rubies, which have been stolen four times, so far. But Irma de Pourboire, the famous young actress, is not superstitious.

DEAR BEACHCOMBER,

Irma sent for me today, and I found her wringing her hands.
"You remember those famous rubies of mine?" she said.
"The ones that have been stolen four times?" I queried.
"Five," she retorted angrily. "You only said four in your publ – propaganda notes, they've gone again – making six times in all."
"Gone?" I said.
"Gone," she said. "Stolen."
"This must be hushed up," I stammered.
"Why, you boob!" she shouted in her distress, "what do you mean?"
"If anyone knows," I said, "detection will be difficult. The thief will be warned."
"Detection my foot!" she cried scornfully, and with great vigour. "Can't you see we must get it known? It's a great chance. A man is said to have – I mean, a man snatched them from my neck last night while I was dancing. He disappeared in the crowd."
"Oh," I said.

"How do you mean 'Oh'?" she said.

"Nothing," I said, "I just said 'Oh'."

It is all very puzzling to me, but I suppose she knows best. I am accordingly enclosing a note about it. I have sent a similar one to the other newspapers, deploring her bad luck.

Yours ever,
O. THAKE

P.S. Tell Saunders to send me a list of all plays with leading parts to be produced in the near future.

CRUEL LARCENY

Miss Irma de Pourboire, the beautiful and brilliant famous young actress, has once more lost her famous and costly rubies, a gift of friendship, one understands, from a noted Indian Rajah to her great-great-grandmother, at the time of the Mutiny. This is the sixth time the beautiful and famous Irma de Pourboire has lost her renowned and celebrated jewels, a family heirloom of priceless antiquity. The gems were stolen from her neck by an international criminal, the leader of a gang well known to Scotland Yard and the French Foreign Office, while she was dancing with a duke. Irma de Pourboire, the famous young beauty, is prostrate with grief, and can make no statement. "I cannot understand it," she said to me after the wanton and cruel larceny.

O. THAKE

DEAR BEACHCOMBER,

A strange individual called on Irma de Pourboire today, while I was busy writing an article about her love of old-world gardens, which I am trying to place with *Our Feathered Cousins and Winged Things Argus*. He produced from a paper bag the famous rubies, and to our startled inquiries he explained that he had found the thief.

"I shall not prosecute," said Irma de Pourboire, magnanimously offering him a cigarette.

"How about the reward?" I said.

Irma looked at the man, and he winked.

"That's all right," he said. "All settled. Does the gent know?" he asked Irma.

"Of course," she snapped, angrily.

All this is very mystifying to me, and later Irma said that he had found them too quickly, and spoilt the story. Does not this show her simple nature? Dear me, it is not every day one meets a mind like untrodden snow.

Rumour is coupling her name with most of the wealthy and titled people here, which is only natural. Letters continue to pour in from managers, but she doesn't let me see any of them, as she says modesty would make her blush at the compliments they pay her. Is she not sweet and gentle?

After dinner last night a man came up to her and said, "Do you want me to go on writing those letters?" She drew him aside in her tactful way, and I heard him say something about having no more London postmarks or English stamps left. I asked her afterwards what it was all about, and she told me he was a man who loved her so much that he pretended to write from England to make her homesick. What devotion! But she is worthy of it – every ounce of it.

Yours,
O. Thake

P.S. Tell Saunders I asked for a list of plays with leading parts, not an out-of-date catalogue of gun-metal fittings. The careless fool!

I have received the following letter from a well-known theatrical manager and producer:

DEAR SIR,

I take it that you are responsible for the deluge of ridiculous literature that is being sent daily to my office. If it is a joke, it is in very bad taste. I am a busy man, and I must protest against this ill-advised pestering. I was always ready to laugh at the adventures of Mr Thake, having believed him to be a creature of your brain, but I think it is going a little too far to arrange for some real person to take his name and become a public nuisance. I am sure that the readers of the *Daily Express* prefer to think of you as a humorist, and not as one who abuses his position as a journalist to play practical jokes. The despatch of this literature from a French resort, all neatly typed, is an ingenious idea, but I must beg of you to carry it no further, as I do not wish to bring the matter before your editor, with, perhaps, unpleasant results for you.

Yours, etc.

DEAR BEACHCOMBER,

The campaign is not successful enough. No paper but the *Daily Express* seems to be taking any notice of this genius in exile, the witty and popular young actress, Miss Irma de Pourboire. I can't understand it. But she is so sweet when I apologize. She said yesterday that she often thought of sacrificing her career, brilliant though it be, and marrying the man of her choice. She would love to settle in an old country manor, which shows how simple and beautiful she is at heart.

"What kind of man would you marry?" I asked.

"He must be English," she said, "and a gentleman. Money is nothing to me, provided we are comfortably off. After all, my garden and my car, and the fun of giving shooting-parties and things, would soon be a substitute for histrionic glory."

That last phrase is, of course, mine, as I have prepared her words for publication, and she is too simple to affect literary turns of speech.

"Tell me," she said, "I should imagine you are in that station of life, are you not?"

I assented as modestly as I could, and she asked what make my car was, and where my country house was, and why I never thought of marriage.

"There," I said, "you tread on mournful soil. One loves but once, and the wound leaves a yawning chasm in the breast of the recipient. I, too, have known Cupid, but to me he was gall and bitter aloes."

"Poor boy," she said in a low voice. "Did it hurt?"

"It cut me," I replied, "to my soul; but memory must begone. Life is life."

"How true," she said, and her sighs mingled with mine.

Her sympathy swept me off my feet, and I patted her head as a father might pat his favourite daughter.

"Little girl," I said, "you are on the threshold of life. See that it does not hurt you. Find a real man to shelter you from the storm."

"I wonder," she murmured, "I wonder where I shall find him?"

"He will roll up, dear lady," I said, "when fate ordains."

"But will he know that I love him?" she queried.

"He will read the tender message in your features," I said. "But till he comes the great public needs you, actress of actresses."

The light faded, and we sat on together, and as I heard her dove-like voice I wondered if ever some woman might not mean to me all that Honoria – ah! that name! – once meant.

"It might be you, blind stranger," she said suddenly.

"What might?" I interrogated.

But she rose swiftly and passed from my ken. I would rather cut off my feet than offend her. Oh, dear!

There is in true friendship a something which it is impossible to describe, and little did I know what a storehouse of warmth is the heart of a real woman until I was privileged to be the chosen friend of the famous and brilliant young actress Miss Irma de Pourboire. She asked me to pretend I was giving her an audition the other day, and she recited to me "Recessional," and "Break, Break, Break," and a speech from "Romeo and Juliet". I wonder some manager does not build her a theatre and commission people to write plays for her.

She warned me today that her stay was drawing to a close. "I shall swoop down on one of these offers that keep arriving by post," she said. "I may take it into my head to accept quite a small part, out of pure whim."

Isn't that delightful? How many other leading actresses would do that?

I shall miss her very much when she is gone. I feel drawn to her, as by a powerful magnet, and were I younger I might easily mistake the blissful urge of friendship for the more tempestuous call of that which makes the world go round. The wildest follies enter my head, as when last night she said she had a crumb in her eye, and bade me remove it. For one second I thought I should imprint upon her white forehead the kiss of adoration, but the moment passed and I flicked with my handkerchief instead. Thus do our dreams come hurtling to *terra firma*.

Irma! What music is the name, as harps twanged softly by candlelight. Thake, Thake, you are not a boy! Stick to your propaganda.

Editors are returning my accounts of her, and they have not even published her photo, under which I have written, "A particularly beautiful studio portrait of that most beautiful, famous, talented, and young of all actresses, the one and only Irma de Pourboire, the public's idol, the profession's despair, the meteor, the comet, the wisp of gold." That last thing she gave me. She said they called her that when she played a dancing girl in Cromarty, and I can well believe it. More power to Cromarty's elbow, say I.

Yesterday she called me Thakey-Wakey! Can ecstasy go further?

Really! I am quite bowled over. It was like this. Last night I saw Irma again and she spoke of leaving the place soon, and asked me if I should miss her.

"Ask the moon," I replied, "if it misses the stars. Ask the earth if it misses the sunshine."

Whereupon she tapped my knee, and said, "Are you serious?"

To which I replied, "I am no trifler."

She then gave me a flower from her dress, and, though it was but a paper one, I swear it seemed to have more scent than any other flower in the world.

"Perhaps," she said, lowering her eyes with that gesture that endears her, I am sure, to her audiences, "Perhaps you will want to say something to me before I go."

"How I hate the word 'go'," I cried.

"Thakey-Wakey," she said, "can't you see — ?"

"Nay," I replied, "I am blinded by your rays."

Her mood changed rapidly.

"You precious dunderhead! You dear little block of wood!" she said, original even in terms of endearment.

"A woman cannot speak," she said, mysteriously, meaning, I suppose, that she was a little moved by my worship of her.

With a long-drawn "Ah," I left her to compose myself.

Dear me, dear me! Am I then desired, and fated at last, after passing through years of troubled water, to weather the storm and win a haven at last? Can it be that she cares for me — me —

unworthy though I am of her lightest word? I must think, I must think. I must not rush in where I was once fool enough not to fear to tread. Angel, angel that she is, and I a dull lout, not fit to buckle her shoe for her. Tomorrow I must try to plumb the depths of her mind, and find out if there is hope. Hope! What a word! Did I but dare to think – ! But, there.

Yours ever,
O. THAKE

P.S. Tell Saunders to explain the heavy bill for clothes-horses. Is he mad?

DEAR BEACHCOMBER,

I write to you in perturbation, hardly knowing whether I am on my hands or my feet. Once more fate has made a sport of me, and the cup has been dashed rudely from my lips. Am I always destined to clutch at the last straw which ultimately breaks the camel's back? Am I never to enjoy what others possess? Why am I always selected to be a joke and a laughing-stock in the hour of my apparent triumph? No. The stars, in their cruel courses, are against me, and once more I must taste alone the bitterness of defeat and humiliation. And I trusted her! Oh, woman is a mockery, and bites off the hand out-stretched to her in adoration. False were her smiles, false as counterfeit coins, and her soft words were poisonous as fungi – as I now know to my cost.

It will be many a day before I regard a woman again with anything but the glance of a basilisk. I will go my lonely way in future, and sirens shall be vipers to me. Enclosed you will find the letter that dashed my desires, and exposed this "leading actress" for what she is, the hanger-on of a low touring company, out for my money and her own glory. She left the hotel in secret with her bill unpaid, and I found in her room this letter which she had left.

This closes for me one more era of Red Sea fruit and ashes. Never again will I be the play hour of a thing.

Yours ever,
O . THAKE

DEAR KID,

Big news! I've got a job at last as one of the twelve Will-o'-the-Wisps in Seymour Farenough's new dance show, "Make It Snappy". But this is where you come in, Irmie – there's one more Will-o'-the-Wisp wanted, and I've told them I know someone for it. Now we're opening in a week or two at Cleethorpes, so they won't keep it open for more than two days. You must wire acceptance, and make tracks at once. There's no good staying out there, specially as you say you don't think that boob of a gent's going to fall for marriage after all. Just sheer off – he's sure to settle your bill, and chuck the idea of being Mrs Thake. What a simp. he sounds, and fancy him getting your name into the papers. Irmie, don't miss this, as it may lead to chorus work in some big town. So pack your grip and beat it, old dear.

Your old pal,
CONNIE.

P.S. Betty's in the show – a swell part – gets four-ten a week now, and hardly speaks to us poor mortals.

My Dear Beachcomber,

Wherever I go I see her face. I see her face in the sea, in the sky, among the trees, on the sands, on the tablecloth, everywhere. I try to read, but cannot focus my attention. How strange life is. I suppose I ought to read philosophy – Hegel or Kant, or something like that. If I could persuade myself that nothing really is, I think I should be happier. But then, some things obviously are – at least, that is how I see it. I almost feel that I wish she had stayed, even if she had torn the shirt off my back, and pawned my socks. The stars are less bright now she is gone. There's nothing left for them to twinkle for. Their queen and regent is in exile, as I heard a man say at a poetry reading in Bloomsbury once. I wish an earthquake would swallow me. I do indeed. I called her name last night, alone in the billiard-room, and only the marker replied. Do try to control Saunders. At any rate, stop him sending me postcard views of Axminster. I do not see how they help.

Yours ever,
O.THAKE